# AMONG THE LAYERS OF THE LAND

## Stories of People,
## Perspectives, and Place

### Frank Rennie

# AMONG THE
# LAYERS
# OF THE LAND

## STORIES OF PEOPLE,
## PERSPECTIVES, AND PLACE

## FRANK RENNIE

First published in 2024 by Acair
An Tosgan, Seaforth Road, Stornoway, Isle of Lewis, HS1 2SD

www.acairbooks.com
info@acairbooks.com

Text © Prof. Frank Rennie, 2024
Illustrations © Fiona Rennie (sradagcreative.co.uk)
Cover design by Fiona Rennie (sradagcreative.co.uk) for Acair

A CIP catalogue record for this title is available from the British Library.

Printed by Hussar Books, Poland
ISBN: 978-1-78907-160-3

Scottish Charity Regulator
Registered Charity SC047866

By Frank Rennie:

## THE CHANGING OUTER HEBRIDES
Galson and the meaning of Place
(*Winner of the* **Highland Book Prize** *2020*)
ISBN: 978-1-78907-083-5

## 101 USES FOR BALER TWINE
*101 Fuasgladh Air Sreang Na Bèile*
ISBN: 978-1-78907-108-5

All royalties from this book will be donated to
The Linda Norgrove Foundation for the support
of women and children in Afghanistan.
https://lindanorgrovefoundation.org/

# CONTENTS

# Acknowledgements

As with many (most?) books of this sort, I have drawn heavily on my own experiences, and from years of notebooks filled with jottings written during walking the dog or after coffee conversations with friends. Chapters two and four were written in the most convivial circumstances during a week living at Moniack Mhòr, Scotland's creative writing centre, which gave me a residency as part of the reward for winning the Highland Book Prize 2020 with my book *The changing Outer Hebrides: Galson and the meaning of place*. So, in a way, this current book is a continuation of that earlier book and extends those lines of thought about what makes a place 'special'. Earlier versions of chapters eight and nine once appeared in the literary magazine *Northwards Now,* and bits of chapter nine were written (and spoken) in different years for the wonderful *Between Islands* festival which is run through An Lanntair in Stornoway, and which links the people of Shetland, Orkney, and the Hebrides (another involvement that is always a pleasure). Some other bits have occasionally appeared as ideas in guest articles on *The Edge* blog hosted by colleagues at the University of the Highlands and Islands.

My thanks are due to many people for their support in both great and small ways: in particular to David Green and Agnes Rennie for their helpful editorial comments on the whole text. Also, to Murdo MacDonald, Emeritus Professor of History of Scottish Art, Roxane Andersen, the UHI Professor of Peatland

Ecology and Sarah Anne Munoz, UHI Professor of Rural Health. Ben Inglis-Grant shared useful field visits to explain the practical processes of peatland restoration and Christopher Fleet, Map Curator at the National Map Library of Scotland stretched my horizons with his incredible cartographical knowledge. As usual, the staff in Stornoway Public Library were consistently helpful, as was Alex MacDonald at An Lanntair, Stornoway and Rachel Humphries and staff at Moniack Mhòr. As always, intermittent conversations with my friends Dr Finlay MacLeod, John Alexander Smith, Malcolm MacLean, and Frances Nimmo frequently contributed inspiration and information that was both pleasurable and rewarding to pursue.

# Prologue

The premise of this book is very simple but, as you might expect from the title, it is multi-layered in its complexity. The ideas expressed here follow on quite naturally from earlier writing of mine that sought to explore, through the lens of my home village, what it is that makes a location 'special'.[88] An obvious corollary is that the landscape itself, irrespective of its geographical positioning, holds unique and pervasive qualities that influence us all, sometimes in ways that we barely perceive, far less fully understand. For decades I have been captivated by a beguilingly uncomplicated scenario that was described by the author Neil Gunn, who was always a profound and enigmatic writer. He explored a concept in his last novel, *The Other Landscape*,[44] in which he suggested that some people view the physical terrain in a subtle, subliminal, yet cryptic language of personalised interpretation that reveals to them a perspective that is hidden from (most) other observers. Gunn likened this to encountering two different people, both superficially similar, and with whom we exchange similar conversations. We instinctively understand that we like the first person but distrust the second. Why is that? Something in the body language perhaps, or the nuance of the conversation, the evasiveness of the eyes, but it is sufficient to distinguish two apparently identical incidents.

The land is like that too. Very often we see only what we expect to see, or what we are conditioned to see, through our history, culture, upbringing, or educational experiences. What is supposedly obvious to one person seems to be completely hidden from another. The barren landscape of one observer is the intriguing ecological paradise of another. An allegedly 'empty wilderness' in one cultural trope is a landscape that has been forcibly cleared of its inhabitants in the historical narrative of another person. Those emotional interpretations are polar opposites.

This crossover, this shifting and figurative layering of different meanings according to individual observers, and indeed for whole communities, is a rich and complicated way to interpret reality. It almost defies description for, by definition, we cannot see, still less comprehend, that which is hidden from us. Our understanding is based (biased, even), at least in part, on our conditioning, and that provides numerous doorways and pathways to an almost infinite variety of landscapes that exist in parallel, simultaneously, in apparent contradiction. Learning to recognise, reveal, and begin to understand the hidden landscape, is a lifelong activity. Some landscape ecologists have argued that as a working definition of 'landscape' is a terrain with two or more ecosystems (e.g., moorland ecosystem and forest ecosystem) it is necessary to understand how *the whole* landscape integrates and inter-relates in order to manage a healthy environment.[94] Context, as well as content, is important, and looking only at patches of the land, or 'reserves', will only give a partial perspective.

# Prologue

This is true whether we adhere to the observations that can be explained by the empirical evidence of natural science, or by the enjoyable elaborations of creative fiction that can take liberties with reality, and in doing so help to elucidate alternative explanations for it. The literature of Scotland is rich in fiction, poetry, and creative non-fiction that illuminate and elaborate on our relationships with the land.[12] Just sometimes, the counterpoise of fact and fiction can help to expose the concepts and potentialities of both that are hidden in the independent genres.[8] That, in essence, is this book. Any exploration of the world around us is so multi-faceted that an exhaustive, comprehensive description in sufficient detail is hardly achievable: we pick our facts from the remnants of perceived reality, and in doing so, hope to shed some light, some understanding, and some enjoyment, on one small part of the complex whole.

# 1
# The basal layers

## THE STUFF OF THE LAND

Our personal use of language to describe places often betrays
the inner comfort levels of our strangeness or familiarity
with that terrain. What we see is not always what we feel, and
the extent to which the clues are visible, let alone obvious or
uncontested, is not always apparent. The hidden landscape,
by which I mean the innumerable layers of meaning and ways
of describing the land in order to better understand it, can
vary widely from place to place, from age to age, and from

person to person. The terrain that we look out across changes from being a space to a place in response to the interactions that people (and other species) have with it. The insights that Scottish writer Neil Gunn speculated upon in his final novel, *The Other Landscape*,[44] and North American writer Barry Lopez described as the links between the visible and the invisible landscape which are only shared in communal association,[56] do not give up their secrets easily. This is precisely why our personal 'special places', when (and if) we find them, frequently appear to have a mysterious spirit of the place that is independent of our being there, but is actuated only by our engagement with that location. It can be so strong an association that it remains with us when we leave that place, almost as an intrinsic property of our experience. In the worldview of the livestock farmer, we are hefted to that place.

One of the indelible marks of a good, comprehensive training in geology is having the ability (indeed it can be almost an unbidden visceral reaction) to make an immediate appraisal about the character of a place simply by looking at the evidence of the terrain. Wherever we are in the world, whichever rural landscape we look upon, geoscientists subconsciously make an almost instantaneous assessment about the stuff that we are standing upon. It is not just the conspicuous, large-scale, surface features that drive these assessments. Certainly, we often look first at the dominant shapes of the landscape, the crags and valleys that determine the configurations of river catchments, or the large-scale humps such as eskers of sand and gravel or lenticular blobs of boulder-clay that are the signatures of later planetary re-working. It is much more than these obvious features, however, as any serious consideration will include many subtle hints at the varieties of solid rock that often lie buried beneath our feet, because these will determine the topography, the derived soil, and in some aspects they may even reflect the human culture of the place.

This analysis is further complicated (and enhanced or confused, depending on your perspective) by the need for the geological scientist to consider the *terrane* of the place - the four-dimensional block of the solid Earth that extends in time over the area of the loose surface deposits downwards towards the mantle and the core. That fourth, additional aspect, is important in any consideration; firstly, the requirement to consider deep time, that sometimes mind-boggling fourth dimension of earth science that changes everything but paradoxically remains the same. Secondly, there are hidden elements of physical places that are not obviously visible (to most people) but which are real, measurable, and immensely important in any attempt to truly understand the history, the significance, and the essence of any specific place. These are often only discernible over long periods of time. To begin with, however, there is much that can be learned from careful first observations.

From my study window, a very obvious feature of the land of the Outer Hebrides is the kilometre after kilometre of dry-stone walls that mark out the boundaries of villages and individual crofts. To many people, they are simply a picturesque element, or perhaps simply a functional part of the overall view. To anyone with a geological inclination, however, there is an instant recognition that these rough, irregular boulders constructing the walls are formed of ancient Lewisian Gneiss. Even within the apparent sameness of the 'undifferentiated gneiss' (i.e., rock so old and convoluted that there are scantily few clues as to its pre-metamorphosed parent rock type) the practised eye picks up the pink splash of a pegmatite or the smooth folds of metasediments that will give clues to the tectonic history of that place. Although we tend to brand it all (by virtue of its Precambrian age) as 'Lewisian Gneiss' the constituent rock formations can vary widely from Archean granite to the twisted and bent remnants of sandstone basins (and every rock type in between). The physical effect of this landscape is an intimate connection between form, function, and environmental history that conveys a particular sense of each unique location. True, the geology alone is not the total 'sense of place', but it is a major modifying factor of the natural environment that conditions so much else, and even at first glance, it influences the landforms, drainage, opportunities for vegetative cover, and much else.[76]

More than that, whenever we travel to another part of the world, a different set of geological identifiers will trigger their own cryptic messages. In Caithness, the stone walls are nothing like those in the Hebrides, having instead, large rectangular slabs of 'flagstone' standing upright on their thin edges, almost like large tiles. On some of the older buildings, especially large flagstones the size of a family dining table may form the main elements of a roof, conveying an impressive gravitas and solidity to the history of previous human occupation. If you are especially diligent, and also especially lucky, you might find, among the accumulated layers of flagstones, the thin dark remains of the fossil fish that singularly identify their provenance and convey specific information on a wealth of Earth history. If we move to Orkney, the field walls are likely to be of red sandstone, while around parts of the Midland Valley, a soft yellow sandstone was favoured for construction. In other regions, like the west of Ireland, the pale local limestone is able to be fashioned into almost-regular blocks that stack solidly with comparative ease. This is a world away from the thrawn, jagged, resilient lumps of Lewisian Gneiss that defy a systematic fracture and will take craft and cunning to fashion into self-standing structures. Additionally, in my own village of Gabhsann, there are a few field walls constructed in a style more commonly found in the Borders region of Scotland, which is a legacy to the old days of the post-clearance Galson Farm, when the grieve (the overseer or head-workman) had originally come from the Borders.

Even in areas where the underlying geology is buried, where the surface of the land is not partitioned by walls of natural stone to provide clues to the tectonic foundations, that landscape speaks to me of its deficits. In the flatlands, or in the regions of the valley floodplains, simply walking alongside a river course is to have the eyes drawn to the shingle, the rolled boulders, and perhaps even some protruding bedrock. Whatever is exposed to your gaze gives an indication of what may be still concealed in that landscape. Whether it is the suggestions given by the loose materials, such as gravels and pebbles, that have been transported from further upstream, or the resistant sliver of a rock-shelf that has been cut by persistent river action, they all have a story to tell about what that place is made of. With a little 'inside knowledge' (pardon the pun!), the details of the three-dimensional terrane are implicit from the superficialities gleaned from a briefly observed perspective of the surface terrain. Even a large and incongruous rock-type, carelessly dumped in apparent isolation, may suggest a glacial erratic, whose close examination might provide clues to both its original source area, and perhaps also the vectors and actions of the moving ice that once sculpted the surface. The directions of glacial striae - scratch marks on the solid rock of the country - can be meticulously recorded and mapped to provide a graphical record that can reconstruct the geography of the last major ice-flow. Those fragments of geological evidence that are scattered around on the surface of the land are mentally accumulated by the geologist, frequently subliminally, and are used to create a mental image of both the deep Earth, and the longitudinal history of why the surface of that place looks as it does.

In addition to rock types like Lewisian Gneiss, Torridonian Sandstone, or perhaps Rhynie Chert, that have been named after the location where they were first scientifically described, there are others that are less well-known in geological nomenclature, and almost entirely unknown to the non-geological public. There are some forms of rock that have such specific and unusual combinations of minerals, or the geochemical presentation of those minerals, that the very fabric of the land is named after the place. Therefore, we have rocks like Appinite (a hornblende diorite) from Appin, on the west coast of Scotland, and Mugearite (an oligoclase-bearing basalt) from Mugeary in the Isle of Skye. In increasing mineralogical diversity, there is Allivalite from the hill called Allival, in the neighbouring Isle of Rum, Ledmoreite (a garnet-pyroxene nepheline-syenite) named for Ledmore, in Sutherland, and from the Kentallen Quarry near the village of Ballachulish, there is Kentallenite, a local name for a melanocratic (dark) variety of monzonite (similar in appearance to a granite) composed mainly of the minerals olivine, augite, micas, and zoned plagioclase with interstitial alkali feldspar. Benmoreite is named after Ben Mòr (Gaelic for 'the big hill') in Mull; the list goes on… Most visitors walk across these rock forms in blithe unawareness. These are very specific descriptive categories of land, as are a few other obscure examples; for instance, in Norway we find distinctive rocks like Nordmarkite, Lardalite, and (my favourite for its bluey-purple iridescence that make it popular as a facing for shopfronts) the spectacular shimmering Larvikite. The names of these mineral assemblages are so characteristic to those specific places that they have derived their rock name from their geographical location. Not only has the place become descriptive of the rock, but the rock has become descriptive of the place. Despite numerous scientific revisions and systematic reclassifications of the geological nomenclature, many of these highly specific rock names are retained in common use; as in most professions, the very precise terminology is useful to distinguish occurrences of singularly exceptional phenomena. In our language of place, we have literally entered *into* the landscape.

Whether it is the interpretation of Earth history, scene by scene, of an entire continent,[77] or simply the view from the back garden, the clues to the fundamental shape and appearance of the land are in those foundations. For better or for worse, our interpretations of the geology of a place are integral to our perceptions of a 'sense of place' and consequently (ultimately) to our understanding(s) of that place. Whether we are thinking about an idealised 'cultural landscape' in our collective national psychology, or the pragmatic details of land ownership and land-use policies,[102] a consideration of the geology of the land is an essential component. For some people, that consideration may be superficial or transitory, for others it will be fundamental. Either way, geological knowledge informs us all about how we see a place. I have found several hand axes made of local quartzite in the ruins of the Mesolithic village along the coast, and they have different meanings for me and for the people who fashioned those cutting-edged tools and used them here three thousand years ago. In other parts of the Gàidhealtachd (the fragmented areas of the Highlands and Islands of Scotland where Gaelic is the cultural root of the indigenous communities) there are known to be stones in the landscape that have been used as natural gongs, so-called 'Singing Stones',[85] although the forms of music that they were used for, and the significance of those rituals, can now only be matters of informed speculation. Singing Stones are less obvious in the landscape than the more ostentatious standing stones, such as Calanais, or the Ring of Brodgar, or even the enigmatic Pictish monoliths with their carved symbols, but all these stones are *of the land*, and they all have different meanings for the many generations of humans who have observed them.

Sometimes, you might notice the landmarks formed by the solitary gable of a ruined croft-house or a shieling, or by the precisely-situated trophies represented by an *ailmh,* a prominent boulder that marks the boundary of the new crofts like our own, placed there to divide the landscape when the crofts were created by breaking up what used to be the larger entity of Galson Farm. The seemingly solid drystone walls that drape over the land for many kilometres, even in this single village, are actually graphic reminders of a time of great fragility and backbreaking labour for ordinary people. The story of this land documents a legacy of contest and conflict.[42]

In most parts of the world, the deep geology is obscured from direct observation by a surface covering of soil and vegetation, and our knowledge of those hidden substrates needs to be pieced together from whatever scant facts that we can glean. There can be few places, however, with such a contrast as that view from my study window. The basal terrane of the Hebridean islands is ancient gneiss, an obdurate, contorted, many-times altered stone that yields its constituent minerals only reluctantly, and even then, parsimoniously. The landscape dominated by Lewisian Gneiss is superficially easy to explain, but to fully understand it requires patience, experience, and insight. I have colleagues who have worked for decades on unravelling the history of its formation over a few square kilometres of land, hoping that they may make a breakthrough and understand a little more. Sometimes they do, and sometimes...

In this small village alone can be found several three-dimensional slivers of land that betray the previous existence of highly diverse geological beginnings, from metamorphosed sediments to meta-volcanics. Literally, entirely separate continents have been welded together and forced to become fellow travellers throughout the subsequent three thousand-million-year history of this wedge of land. As I walk my regular routes along a section of the coast that buffers our township from the vagaries of the Atlantic, there is a short section where possibility and probability collide in deep geological time, and I (with the eye of faith) believe I can detect a protolith - a small lens of the older, original, rock of this planet, encased in younger gneiss. Considering that around 3,500 million years have passed since the formation of this enveloping bedrock of 'younger gneiss', which itself is almost 2000 million years older than the almost identical gneiss a few kilometres further northeast in Nis, this protolith may have its origins of formation around 4,000 million years before I first saw it exposed to the sun. In one sense, simply walking along the shoreline of the village is an exercise in time travel.

## THE CLOAK OF PEAT

In complete contrast to the bare, exposed bedrock, the blanket covering that masks almost the entire Hebridean inland landscape, frequently to a depth of several tens of metres, is so young that it is still growing and accumulating, yet paradoxically is mostly dead. In a sense, that is perhaps not quite so strange. Like so many other aspects of landscape ecology, the accumulation of peat is very simple in concept, but almost infinitely complex in reality. If there is any mechanism through which this land could in any way be described as 'hidden' then the formation of peat must surely have a key part in that process. The accumulated layers of peat overlying the solid rock, with the depth increasing over the whole land surface area by perhaps barely a millimetre a year, could be considered as simply layer upon separate layer of organic matter. As the surface vegetation dies, the waterlogged ground beneath it inhibits the activity of the microorganisms that would normally decompose organic material into soil, and so the dead plants simply pile up. While the topmost few centimetres retain a recognisable similarity to fibrous heathland turf, the bottom zone, squeezed by compaction from above, is turned into a smooth, dense, clay-like texture, and dries to a black, brittle consistency that burns almost like coal, with an intense heat. It might take a team of two people a single, long day, to cut by hand enough peat to maintain a household in fuel for a whole year. (Peat, we say, warms you three times; once when you are cutting it, again when you take it home, and finally when you burn it). In the communities where families traditionally burn peat as a fuel, every stage of the process, every part of the peat bank, each individual layer of cut peats, has a name and a purpose, producing an entire cultural lexicon.[15] The black *caoran* from the base produces a fierce heat for cooking on the stove, the *bàrr-fhàd*, the lighter cut from the top of the bank, is useful to smoor a fire in the hearth overnight, yet still has enough embers to rekindle it the following morning. The land has multiple uses, and therefore multiple meanings and multiple ways to engage with it.

There is a wonderful phrase in Gaelic - *falach-fuinn*, an activity which Dwelly's dictionary translates as '*land-hiding; taking advantage of every natural feature in the landscape to hide themselves.*'[31] Probably the term derives from hunting activities, but there is the possibility of something more clandestine, the anticipation and expectation of the need to travel unobtrusively across a potentially hostile terrain. As an example of a 'hidden' landscape, of countryside filled with subtly diverse meanings and interpretations, peatland is the choice par excellence. Every time you look at it, each visit and every scrutiny from a distance, there is something different in your scope.[55] We may not always notice that difference, for it might just be the movement of an animal that wishes to remain unnoticed, or it might be a minuscule change in the vegetation, responding to the sun, the wind, or the changes in the water table, but those changes are important. They are significant for the moorland landscape, for its ecology, and consequently for every species that interacts with that peatland habitat, including you and me.[84] In addition to its recreational benefits, undisturbed peatland is essential for crucial ecosystem services such as water purification, flood alleviation, biodiversity,[93] and as we have discovered in the last couple of decades, as a vital carbon storage facility to help regulate global climate change.[7] The oxygen-poor ground conditions slow the decomposition of dead plant material, and as organic matter piles up, its carbon content is retained within the peat. Sphagnum moss, a significant component in the vegetational communities of many peat moorlands, can hold substantial quantities of water, and yet 50% of its dry matter weight is carbon.

There are many species of sphagnum mosses, and every one of them occupies a distinctive niche in the ecosystem. The species differ in their rates of production and decay; they vary in their colour, hydraulic conductivity, depth of formation, hummock structure, and their associated invertebrate life. When you look at each layer of a depth of peat, you are looking at an ancient land surface that has been steadily buried beneath the vegetation of subsequent land surfaces. Under the microscope, thousands of millions of pollen grains, appearing like grotesque macro-bacteria, spiky and globular, ovoid, triangular, and distorted, provide a detailed record of the millennia of species abundance and the genetic variety of vegetative growth.[5] The very fine volcanic ash that was ejected by historical eruptions in Iceland was carried by the wind and deposited across the land surface of Northern Europe. The ash lay on the surface of the land, and in places was eventually covered by more layers of peat. These buried layers of ash, too fine to be distinguished by the naked eye, delineate the horizon of previous landscape surfaces, now altered. The precise dating of each eruption event enables scientists to correlate widely spread localities to provide a snapshot of contemporaneous landscapes, and to back-calculate the changes in vegetation and bog moisture as a result of climate changes.[51] A four-dimensional perspective of landscape begins to become visible, changing with time asynchronously across the countryside.

Thanks to the deep accumulation of plant remains, peatlands are highly effective terrains for storing carbon, one of the key elements in the atmosphere driving global climate change, as well as, ultimately, human nature and our relationships with the land.[75] Estimates of the current extent of northern peatland vary, but it could be as much as 346 million hectares containing 455 billion metric tons of carbon,[17] so there is a great deal of interest not just in protecting the remaining intact peatland ecosystems, but also in the repair and restoration, where possible, of peatland that has already been subjected to human disturbance.[30] As a dominant plant species of healthy moorland, sphagnum mosses are a crucial building component of any restorative activities. Sphagnum retains water in its structure, and this affects the level of the water table across the land by soaking up or releasing groundwater and precipitation. From my colleague, Roxane Andersen, I learned of the concept of 'bog breathing'. As the layers of a peat bog dry, the bog shrinks slightly; as it becomes wetter, for example during winter, it expands. This happens in regular cycles, and incredibly these oscillations are measurable from space.[70] Although it has only been established relatively recently, this regular bog surface oscillation could be a useful indicator of the ecological integrity of a bog, and also a potential tool to help plan the restoration of damaged areas of peatland in order to help mitigate the effects of climate change.[50]

The landscape is changing before our eyes, although the speeds of the changes are often out of sync with human cycles of perception.[21] Too slow or too fast, and the change is accomplished, frequently irreversibly, before we ever notice that there is a problem. Over 80% of UK peatlands are considered to be in a degraded state; in Germany it is 95%.[7] Some historically classic peatland landscapes have gone forever, others are fragmented and modified almost beyond recovery.[17] Although the north Lewis moor is one of the largest and most ecologically intact peatland areas in Europe, it is more of a managed landscape than the 'wilderness' portrayed in the populist media. As might be expected, the recolonisation of damaged moorland proceeds slowly, and different species bounce back differentially, so there is a developing branch of science and technology that is emerging to understand and attempt to address the myriad problems that this presents.[1]

To satisfy my curiosity, on a lovely July day, I went to visit the moor around Loch Orasaigh, with Ben, a peatland ecologist. There is a growing interest, these days, in restoring damaged peatland, and Ben is responsible for managing and monitoring a number of pilot sites in the Isle of Lewis. I had read about the theory of restoration, and I wanted to see the practical aspects. Around the area of this pilot site, test cores have established the depth of peat to vary between 0.5 and 3 metres. Part of the area contains old peat banks that are now disused, while other parts are bare surfaces of black peat, dusty, drained, and exposed to further erosion by wind and rain. It is still in the early days of the pilot, and the full restoration of a vibrant peatland habitat will require decades of management, not simply a few years, but the initial results are encouraging. The trenches caused by the peat cuttings have been 'profiled' (i.e., the turf has been pulled back, the drops and ditches smoothed over, and the turf covering re-laid) with the result that it is often difficult to register where the original peat banks lay. Old drains have been blocked to allow the water table to rise and re-wet dried-up areas, encouraging the regeneration of native vegetation. In other locations, sphagnum is grown offsite, for subsequent transplantation into damaged areas to help speed up the recolonisation of appropriate plant communities.[38] If this pilot work is successful, it holds a fantastic potential to re-establish degraded peatland ecosystems and at the same time mitigate global environmental problems. Although superficially similar in appearance, there are subtle but crucial differences in the range and abundance of species that are supported in the restored areas in comparison with pristine peatland habitats. To the uninitiated, landscapes can look identical, but the comparative biodiversity tells a totally different story. Ben took an obvious pride in pointing out the flat expanses of white-flossed native *Canach* (Cottongrass) waving in the gentle breeze; it's a small beginning, but it's a start. Yet, a short distance away, on a small island in a loch, where grazing sheep and deer cannot reach, the entire land surface is thickly dominated by trees and shrubs, creating a small patch of an entirely different ecosystem. The study of some gorges in the West Highlands of Scotland necessitated the creation of an additional category of land classification, because the unique combination of species coexisting in localities with such natural protection was not replicated even a few hundred metres away. We are still slowly discovering those exotic combinations of vegetational communities and learning to understand the fine balances in landscape ecology that enable a species to thrive, or simply to survive in adverse circumstances.

Once, walking far out on the hill with a friend, we were enjoying our day outside, it was warm but not hot, a moist freshness in the air but not damp, when suddenly, within a few minutes, a thick, impenetrable mist came down. It did not worry us unduly, although the speed of it caught us by surprise, for we were familiar with the curves of the place, so we walked on, continuing to chat as we moved slowly through the greyness. After half an hour or so, the mist thinned slightly, and we stopped in astonishment. We had thought that we knew exactly where we were, no need for compass or GPS here, but incredibly, we were looking across the broad, open-topped V of a shallow mountain valley, - a *feòran* - perhaps a kilometre wide, with a meandering river in the lower apex, five hundred metres below us, spread out like a map in perspective. We realised that we had no idea where we were! As we stood for a few seconds in puzzlement, each of us trying to reorient our sense of geography, the mist rose a little higher, and what it revealed was even more astonishing. We were exactly where we had thought we should be. The broad 'valley' in front of us was no more than a dip in the moor, three metres across and a couple of metres deep, with the 'river' a laughable trickle, scarcely three centimetres wide. Suddenly, clarity was restored to the landscape, and a useful lesson was learned, but not before generating some heart-thumping confusion. The human brain is exceedingly complex, and this allows us to balance different versions of reality. If a human face needed to be *precisely* the same in order to recognise it again, we would be in real trouble when that person smiled, or frowned, or simply had a tiring day. Within certain limits, we learn to tolerate deviations from that first vision, what Bronowski termed The Principle of Tolerance.[10] We see landscapes like this too, even if we don't realise it. Although the mist had tricked us, when it had cleared completely, I was left with a dreamlike sensation, as if we had suddenly re-emerged from a faraway country. In one way, we had.

## Consuming the land

We are accustomed to consuming the products of the land, the vegetables, the grains, some berries, even indirectly (via the grazing animals) the grasses, rushes, and heathers, but not, usually, the land itself. The timber and the crops, we almost take for granted as natural entitlements that are available for the taking and the labour of harvesting, but what about the land in its entirety? There is perhaps an assumption that the land surface is relatively unchanging from generation to (human) generation, wearing away only a millimetre at a time. Classic landscape photographs are sometimes compared with current views, and the minuscule differences commented upon with delighted recognition. Even when the 'product' is the abundance of scenic views for the tourist, the terrain is commoditised and categorised. There is an impression, however, that the land itself has a solidity that is the same barely changing perspective for all observers, but is it?

Apart from reshaping the ground and modifying the vegetative layers, in specific localities the land itself is sometimes consumed. In stone and gravel quarries, the surface of the land is modified and relocated. Rocks are exploded, pulverised, and re-used in other locations to build new roads, buildings, harbours, and bridges. Whole mountains can be reconfigured. This, to be accurate, entails more than just moving the office furniture around into a new arrangement. There are scarcely perceptible nuances that influence whether a quarry is regarded as a bountiful gift of natural resources or an eyesore that is a blight on the land. When the proposal is to excavate a superquarry and remove an entire mountain, as was once suggested for the ice-scraped hill of Roineabhal, in South Harris, then mere economic opportunism can be eclipsed and shamed by the public recognition of deeper emotional, almost visceral ties with the physical presence of the land. Even people who until now have scarcely given the shape of the land, or the content of the ground, a passing consideration, begin to realise the emotive power of those subliminal connections.[74] A more profound awakening is uncovered, and something precious and rare, yet strangely familiar is made manifest. It is involuntary. We see the land in different and frequently changing ways.

For many visitors to the islands, the honeycombed walls of hand-cut peat present an almost iconic image of the Hebridean moorland. To locals, the image is less romantic and more pragmatic, but nevertheless intimately associated with our attitudes towards this landscape. In many crofting communities peat is still cut each year as fuel for the hearths and stoves, to help warm and feed people. Peat cutting has never been on the commercial scale, as in Ireland and Russia, that has been so environmentally destructive in those countries, and even the current domestic cutting is a fraction of the historical activity. This is an individual relationship with the moor, household by household, in which crofts have associated traditional areas, allocated by agreement with the community, that have been worked over generations. A small portion is removed each year that is subsequently transported home and used to sustain and comfort the family throughout the year. Neil Gunn once wrote,

> *"The smell of peat smoke was thick and cosy. It had a social warmth. A whiff of it today, caught as a car hurtles along a Highland road, is enough to evoke at once a whole way of life."* [45]

Only someone who has never had to make the (several days') effort to clean, cut, throw, haul, and stack a few hundred metres of dense peat will tell you that peats are a 'free' fuel. To the rest of us, the heritage of peat cutting is another way of seeing the landscape, part ritual, part celebration, and partly an economic harvest as simple as farming.

In a curious way, the power that the peatlands have provided these communities for centuries is morphing into other forms of exerting power. With both the growing sophistication of wind turbines and the nascent potential of carbon capture to mitigate at least some aspects of climate changes, peatland is acquiring a new value. Extending far beyond the provision of the superficial (but important) benefits for outdoor recreation, a landscape that was once routinely categorised as 'barren' is now becoming viewed with a heightened sense of environmental awareness. This is exactly the same landscape, but with a diametrically opposed evaluation of its worth.

If you have ever spent any length of time on an open peatland habitat, either working in the peats or simply walking among the myriad *dubh lochan* (black peat-pools) you may have noticed the reflections of a multi-coloured seepage across the surface of a calm pool of water. Far removed from any traffic or industrial activity, oil stains in peat pools, exhibiting a glistening opalescence reminiscent of the colour of the inside of mussel shells, glimmer under the rays of the sun. As a direct result of this phenomenon, one of the most bizarre interludes of the industrial revolution unfolded amidst the Lewis moors.

The restless economic enthusiasm (and disregard for environmental ethics) of the Victorians helped to drive the industrial and scientific explorations of the mid 1800s. One of the unlikely avenues for exploitation was bankrolled by Sir James Matheson, the new 'owner' of the Isle of Lewis who, having made an almost incredible fortune from the Opium Wars in the Far East, was now attempting to establish himself as an enlightened politician who was, "*attached to science and anxious to promote its progress*".[107] For several years Matheson supported an initiative to distil the oil from peat on a grand scale, to supply lamp lighting oil, lubricants for machinery, and anti-fouling tar for shipping. At one point the Lewis Chemical Works included nearly fifty miles (eighty+ kilometres) of moorland peat banks that were being harvested at the edge of Stornoway, burning at its peak around one hundred tons of peat per week, to produce high quality liquid paraffin oil and candle wax on a commercial scale that surprised everyone, including the main promoters. At full production, there were several hundred employees in three geographically separate manufactories, with ten large distillation kilns, a works canal, and an extensive tramway to transport the raw materials. Ultimately, the enterprise collapsed in an inglorious confusion, not because the product manufacturing process was unsuccessful, but through a toxic cocktail of circumstances, including local mismanagement, financial irregularities, and disruptive world markets that simply could not compete with the new world order. After a brief flash in the headlines of political opportunity, the peatlands of Lewis retreated into a comfortable obscurity.

# 2
# The hidden layers appear

SOMETIMES IT REQUIRES FICTION TO PEEL
BACK THE LAYERS THAT WE CAN ONLY IMAGINE.

The whole land appeared new-washed and sparkling after
the early-morning rain, as if it was just being created anew,
which in a sense, it was. There was a freshness in the air and
a cool, welcome breeze that discouraged the insects. Ae-lee
wandered slowly inland beside the stream; her mother had sent
her to collect some of the sticky red clay to make pottery and
figured that her daughter could not get lost walking alone as

long as she could follow the stream home. Along the coast, her father and his brother had gone looking for food, and though she knew that she held a special place in her father's affections, she also knew that she would not have the stamina to keep up with their movements. They each had jobs to do, and because Ae-lee had been to the clay place before, with her mother and her aunt, she knew where to find the riverbank spot. She thought that she would have plenty of time, so there was no need to rush. She had enough time to include her own projects. When she was certain that her brothers were not following her, she dropped down to an area of bare rock that surrounded a series of boulder-strewn pools. With a final furtive look around, to make sure that she was not being watched, Ae-lee pulled a small skin bag from beneath her clothing and squatted down by the water. In the backwash of the current in a shallow rock-pool, she began to pick carefully, with the infinite patience and dexterity that only a child could muster, the beautiful silvery flakes among the coarse sand. She had no idea what mica was made of, but it looked spectacular, glittering in the morning sun, and she was sure that it must be a valuable commodity to trade. Sparkling like stars in her small hand, it *had* to be a treasure, it was *so* beautiful. It looked like the shiny scales of fish skin, only more precious because these fragments of rock retained their sheen even after the fragments had dried. Her mother would be surprised by this gift. After fifteen minutes of gathering, she had added some weight to the bag and was beginning to tire of the business, so she hid the prize beneath her belt again and washed her hands carefully in the ice-cold stream, squeezing the tell-tale grains of silt from beneath her nails.

Idly, she clambered a little further upstream, then found a dry spot to sit daydreaming in the sun. She noticed a clump of pretty yellow flowers a short distance away, and leaving her bundle beside the water, walked across to pick some of them. There was a larger clump further up the bank and she followed her instincts. Rising out of the slight V in the ground made by the flow of the stream, an extensive scattering of trees was spaced out from horizon to horizon, filling the broad half-bowl shape of the river valley. Beneath the broken canopy and the thin trunks, the interplay of light and shade produced a dappled, dreamlike effect. She was sure that it was magical. Dotted here and there were white flower heads, delightful tattered pink flowers, and swaying patches of white fluffiness that seemed to shimmer in the half-light. The depth of the shadows contrasted to make the lighted world more real. As she stood there, almost transfixed, a small dark butterfly with a bright orange dash on its wing fluttered erratically between the splashes of sunlight. She felt sure that nobody had ever walked among these trees before, she was the very first person. An intoxicating fragrance had filled the air; she would have liked to have known the source, to take it home with her, but as quickly as it had come, the scent vanished. There might be animals hidden in this world, monsters even, but the absolute silence and serenity of the place relaxed her, and the flowers *were* beautiful. It was difficult to imagine anything horrible amidst this beauty. With a nervous backward glance over her shoulder, towards where her bundle of clay stood to betray its abandonment, she gently stepped deeper into the trees, zigzagging from flower to flower. This forest seemed so different to the coastal fringe where the family lived that she felt she was being drawn into this enchanted place.

Later, she snuggled down in a little hollow of dry, spiky grey mosses, and drifted off to sleep, contented with the natural world.

When she awoke, it was with a jump. Instantly alert, she moved not a muscle, but strained her ears to detect the source of her disturbance. Easing her head slowly out of the hollow, she could see two men, walking together, side by side through the trees, but gesticulating as they walked, with angry, raised voices. Fear crept in her chest, and even when she belatedly recognised the speakers, and curiosity had replaced outright fear, the thumping of her heart seemed so loud they should surely hear it, even over this distance. Ae-lee saw that one of the men, the angry one, was her uncle, the younger brother of her mother. The other man, Otan, was a distant relative too, but he was much quieter, seemingly apologetic, but every so often he seemed to be prodded into loud denials and outbursts. Their argument slowly receded into the trees, although occasional loud noises would filter back to her, leaving her confused and intrigued.

Ae-lee liked her uncle, he was always playing games and tricks, but he had a way of discombobulating her. Once, when he had taken Ae-lee and her younger brother rock fishing along the shore, she had watched one of those tricks with the clinically-detached observation of a child. As her brother was temporarily distracted untangling his line, she watched her uncle pull out a dead fish from under his jacket, clip it onto the hook on his line, and throw it into the sea. He then made a big act of pulling it ashore, stamping his feet in the pools and yelling with excitement, deliberately turning the whole performance into a comedy. Her brother had been impressed with the catch, but she knew that it was a lie; she had seen him accomplish the deception right in front of her eyes, but no one ever notices a girl. Her uncle had looked closely at her, squinting sideways with his eyes and a sly inquisitive smile. He suspected that she knew something that she was not sharing, and she had an awareness of his suspicion, but nothing more was said. Through this incident, Ae-lee first became aware of the undercurrents of human character, and the fact that our impressions of people, just like places, can appear to be contradictory to independent observers.

As silence returned to the gathering of trees, a small bird, feathered in slightly different shades of brown, bobbed into view. It danced in the clearing in front of her, coming closer, then moving further away, almost teasing her. In her child's imagination, the bird was coaxing her to follow, and she was immediately superstitious; the bird had emerged from nowhere, was this a good sign or an evil omen? Before Ae-lee had enough time to fully consider this dilemma, a larger bird with a hooked beak came dashing between the trees with a rush of wind. In a second, the larger bird had snatched the small brown bird from the sky. No noise. No fuss. One second it was there and the next it had disappeared, leaving only a few curled little feathers wafting in the breeze to prove that it had ever existed. The suddenness and the brutality unnerved her. Only the memory of the swooping rush of wind and the blur of movement remained, but the spell of the woodland had dissipated. She felt that she needed to be out of that place; at once.

She walked away quickly, not wanting to scare herself further by running, but not wanting to linger, even for long enough to permit proper navigation. With the seed of panic inside her she looked around quickly, randomly, for anything that she recognised, any feature or fragment of her outward journey. But the memories were already hidden in the landscape, and they were not willing to reappear for Ae-lee. Dimly, she followed the land downslope, looking from tree to tree, searching the spaces in between the trees for geographical inspiration, and slowly rationality returned. As the woodland thinned towards the edge, she perceived the final dip of the ground into the river and sat down with a thump on a mound of heather to recover her breath. As her world slowed down to a normal pace, she became aware of someone singing, a light and gentle melody hanging in the air. At first, she imagined that the unreality of the hidden things in the woodland had pursued her, but then realised that the sound was drifting up from the slope below her. Carefully, Ae-lee crept forward, and almost laughed aloud with relief when she saw that the singer was her eldest sister, gathering plants with their mother, who she could now also see, slightly further down the hill. For a moment, Ae-lee had a twinge of jealousy, for she had always wanted to go out searching for medicinal plants with her mother, but she was still regarded as being too young to share the power of that secret knowledge. She watched them for several minutes, foraging among the vegetation where the coastal grassland graded into moorland, then quietly she backed away into the shelter of the scraggly bushes and retraced her steps to reclaim her bundle of red clay. A little later, following the path of the river back to their village beside the beach, she was spotted in the distance by her sister, and they exchanged waves of acknowledgement to join their two worlds.

That evening, as the family clustered around the fire to share their evening meal, someone remarked that it was unusual for Otan to be outside so late that he missed his food. Had anyone seen him? Some inner warning encouraged Ae-lee to remain silent, initially probably to avoid revealing that she had strayed out of the river valley into the forbidden landscape of the woodland. As the darkness of the night came down, and Otan had still not appeared, she became aware of a ripple of unease encroaching into the adult conversation of the group. She hoped that her face showed no traces of surprise when her uncle told them that he had not seen Otan all that day. Ae-lee just knew that she had seen the two of them arguing about something among the trees, and only one of them had returned to the village. Her uncle looked at her quizzically at one point, measuring her up with his strange sideways glance and his sly smile, but she contrived to make herself busy in a corner and the moment passed, though Otan was never seen again.

# 3

# Layers of territory

## VEGETATIONAL NEIGHBOURHOODS

Studying the north Lewis landscape from the air, a mesmerising palette of muted colours and replicated patterns of surface morphology appear to be repeated in infinite botanical combinations of four-dimensional geometry - the spread on the ground and the height above the meagre soil.[82] If we think about it at all we might assume that higher species like birds have adapted to live in communities, but plants, well, plants are just there, aren't they? Any significant awareness is not aided by the familiar linguistic customs of talking about 'seabird cities' and 'colonies' of terns, or gulls, whereas most vegetation, apart from the common, in-your-face flowers, are only ever described by their scientific descriptors. While acknowledging that every specialist subject requires the precision and specificity of its own terminology, the majority of these botanical names do not slip easily off the tongue. (How *do* I pronounce that word? Is the emphasis on the first syllable or the second, or perhaps the third?)

Trichophoreto-Eriophoretum-caricetosum communities (for instance) in oligotrophic (nutrient poor) mires do not normally make a regular appearance in casual, everyday conversation. For the most part, the true identity of plants remains concealed beneath the facade of their names, rendered in the long-dead language of Latin. In addition, there is a complicated terminology required for the description, classification, and comparison of the individual species in similar genera. For example, currently 380 separate species of *Sphagnum* moss, *alone*, are recognised, and are differentiated only by the identification of minutely idiosyncratic distinctions in their morphology, such as leaf shape (spathulate, lingulate, triangular ...), leaf orientation (erect, hanging, spreading, curve ...), and colouration.[48] For 99-point-something percent of people looking at the landscape of peatland, most clumps of moss look pretty similar to any other clump of moss, and the intricacies of their botanical terminology are completely invisible, lost in the landscape. The classic authoritative scientific writing on the plant communities of the Highlands and Islands of Scotland,[78] is a goldmine of fascinating information and helped lay the foundations for contemporary ecology, but for the non-botanically inclined it is a bit like reading a telephone directory. Many of the subsequent scientific papers refining the vegetational classifications are just as likely to confuse your understanding as they are to shed any light. Perusing the pages of species lists, knowledge is gathered, connections are made, and associations can be established, but the *essence* of those habitats, like the landscape itself, is perceived only vaguely, through the drifting mists.[22] The moor is much more complex and also simpler than it appears at first sight, more subtle but also more varied.[41]

The ecosystem of a peat moorland is described by scientists as an example of a complex adaptive system. Generally, we are only aware of a few of the more obvious connections in the millions of interlinked relationships that operate in a healthy bog. Key to the functioning of those relationships are feedback loops, each of which is directly or indirectly linked to every other loop. Positive feedback loops cyclically magnify and tend to accelerate change, whereas negative feedback operates to reduce change and attempts to restore balance. For example, sphagnum moss can hold up to twenty-five times its own dry weight in water, and in waterlogged ground this produces ideal conditions for the growth of more moss to flourish.[3] Frequently the water table - the height of the groundwater in the subsoil - is drawn upwards, slightly nearer the surface, by the sucking action of the mosses. In addition, the mosses make the groundwater more acidic, which discourages competing plants, and this positive feedback favours the further expansion of the moss community, which results in an even more suitable habitat for mosses.

Excavating a new drain, of course, will have the reverse effect by lowering the water table and drying the mosses. It is this wetting and drying process that we can observe in the 'bog breathing' process, but there will be countless other knock-on effects that we do not observe quite so easily. Each plant species coexists with a range of other species that will vary in almost infinite detail, as the impact of the moisture content, soil chemistry, solar radiation, or wind desiccation influences the health of the separate plants. Within each assemblage of plant species there will be an associated community of invertebrates that help in pollination and also regulate the breakdown of dead organic matter. The variety and abundance of the invertebrates will provide food for a community of birds and other animals that forage amongst the mosses. It's complex, and each little cycle of activity is constantly adapting in response to the ceaseless changes of the other cyclical processes. The natural world is in constant motion, interacting as if by magic in multiple dimensions in response to an almost limitless number of factors of change. There is no 'magic', but neither is there any landscape pattern without an underlying meaning.

Yet those plant communities and territories of species are real, they exist, and though they may not appear to be obvious in your personalised landscape panorama, the connections are not hidden from everybody. There are good reasons for those subtle changes in the shades of greens and yellows that pattern the landscape that you observe. Systematic analysis shows that many species of plants like to be lumped together; they may enjoy the companionship of damp hollows, or acidic substrates, they may prefer the drier, well-drained, lime-rich sandy fields. There is a layer of the land in which the vegetational community exists in a relationship of reciprocal benefit and competition. Some plant communities, such as the Hebridean machair grassland, require regular grazing in order to maintain the rich floristic biodiversity as fast-growing species are prevented from overly-dominating other important, yet sensitive and slower-growing species. Regular patterns appear, and within limits the associations can be predicted. There are at least 22,000 species of mosses in the world,[106] yet most humans would be considered skilled to be able to identify more than six. Mosses are the most primitive of land plants, occupying a living space in virtually every known ecosystem, and they have developed fascinatingly complex strategies to cope with almost every extreme threat to their survival, but to all but a small section of the public, they are unnoticed and unregarded. Looking at the landscape of a peatland expanse, I know that an intricate mosaic of vegetational patterns exists, that those communities of plants are finely tuned to their local microenvironments, but I know this from prior experience, not because I can see the self-evident details from where I stand.

I look at the contrasts of light and shade, the gradations of colour, changing throughout the year, and I look closely at the configurations of the land.[53] I make assumptions based on previously acquired knowledge which must be constantly updated and revalidated later in some future ground-truthing visit. In my head, I run through a list of some of the many descriptive terms that people who have inhabited this place before me have given to this land, in their efforts to understand, utilise, and commune with the place. *Aigheannach* (a place where thistles grow), *ansgairt* (a thicket of Brambles), *beacanach* (abounding in mushrooms), *ciobach* (full of Deergrass), *conasgach* (plentiful in Gorse), *fiadh-ghleann* (a wild glen where deer herd together), *gròiseideach* (abounding in Gooseberries), *lusrach* (a place well-supplied with herbs).

The list goes on and on, limited only by my personal awareness of that local knowledge. This does not even begin to include the myriad descriptions of agricultural uses of the land, nor the minute differentiations in the attributes of running water, the distinctive appearances of areas of wet land, (degrees of marshiness), the types of surface texture and structures of landforms. It does not include the terminology that beguiles me as examples of outdated associations with this landscape; *fraon* (a place of shelter in the mountains), *cro-sheilg* (a hiding-place for hunters), *làimhrig* (a natural landing place on the shore). The language exhibits the finesse of the functional engagement of humans with place, a richness that recognises and values the minutiae of difference, because those differences may be of importance one day.

These layers of the landscape are open to a diversity of interpretations: no pattern is without meaning. With practice, discrete areas of distinctive differences appear, and can be categorised in the memory: contrasting colours, intriguing textural features, recognisable shapes. The interaction between species, hydrology (drainage), pH (relative acidity), species movements (grazing pressure), nitrogen levels (guano) - all these factors and more are interconnected. I have even read of the inhibiting impact of sheep paths on the down-slope drainage, caused by the thin band of soil compaction produced by the persistent passage of tiny hooves. Miniscule local differences create a vibrant patchwork of microenvironments, rich in biodiversity. Yet the place has been called 'barren' - or worse, 'a wilderness'. Landscape ecologists have recognised people who have a deep relationship with the land as a fabric of their whole being as 'empathetic insiders',[49] which is in total contrast to the superficial perspective of those whose experience of the peatland is simply as external voyeurs, speeding through the landscape on slender ribbons of tarmac, not engaging, but watching from edges without leaving the comfort of their cars.

## FEELGOOD FLOWERS

You would be forgiven for thinking that your simple stroll around this landscape is a field trip through a pharmacological cornucopia. So many of the innocuous plants that you stomp over have, to a greater or lesser extent, a heritage of medicinal use. An understanding of the use of the natural environment for healing in the context of Gaelic culture lay in the oral tradition, but it is a heritage that has medical links to Islamic and Greek practices and has associations with some of the most ancient European universities.[2] It is true that some herbal concoctions are more efficacious than others, but Bog Myrtle was used as a general remedy to reduce a fever long before the medical properties of quinine were discovered (and it is still utilised as a natural repellent against the dreaded midges of the Highlands and Islands!). Bogbean is still favoured by many people to treat headaches and migraines, and a tincture of Eyebright is recognised as effective relief from sinusitis.[80] A great many of the common plants that are found growing wild on the moor, along the shore, and in the natural grasslands of pasture that are managed in a low-intensity manner, have been used by our ancestors to make dyes for textiles, for spreading on the floor to create pleasant fragrances, and boiled, chewed, or chopped to provide useful health products that were rooted (sorry for the pun,) in the intimate knowledge that our forebears had with the living landscape.

Tormentil is one of my favourite plants, or *Potentilla erecta*, to give its specific scientific name. When I stop to think about why I like this species in particular, I can't quite define it, but there are a number of contributing reasons. It is a low, inconspicuous plant, forming creeping patches of slender stems supporting little toothed green leaves and cheerful, four-petalled, bright yellow flowers, like a scattering of centimetre-sized dots of sunshine among the muted colours of the moor. It is quite widespread in the Highlands and Islands of Scotland, on heathland and grassland, so long as the soil is acidic and not too wet, so its recognition is like meeting an old friend. I also like the fact that it is both attractive and functional, for there are several known uses for this particular layer of vegetation. On a walk with Ben, we paused to admire a clump of Tormentil on a restored area of moorland, and I started to list its historical uses.

Because of the effect of the tannins in its roots, from ancient times until the 1950s, Tormentil was collected and used for tanning leather and in preserving fishing nets and sails from

53

rotting from exposure to saltwater. The roots were boiled in vats and the skins/nets were immersed for treatment. It was said that it would take a person a whole day to dig up enough roots for a single batch, and in order to prevent over-exploitation and habitat damage, some communities restricted its collection.[80] It was also utilised along with Marsh Woundwort (*Stachys palustris*) to produce a yellow dye for textiles. Crucially, Tormentil was favoured as a common medication - the roots were boiled in milk and used to treat diarrhoea and dysentery, as well as, in former years, as a treatment for intestinal parasites. In some parts (for example in South Uist) it was also chewed as a remedy for cold sores, and more recent research has confirmed its antibacterial and anti-inflammatory potential in dentistry.[79]

If this catalogue of therapeutic claims begins to seem like a quack doctor's medicine show, it is worth noting that, since the medieval period at least, the clues to its effectiveness are in the names given to this beneficial little plant. Its generic Latin name, *Potentilla*, means power, which is a direct reference to its perceived value in pharmacology. The common name in English, Tormentil, also has a Latin root - *tormentina*, which means 'intestinal colic', and its name in German is *Blutwurz*, a reference to the red colour, caused by the tannins in the roots, as well as an indication that in bygone times it was regarded as an effective treatment to stop bleeding. Little wonder that it is considered to be an underestimated resource in complementary medicine.

Throughout the peat layer, the steady accumulation of plant debris and pollen grains within the fabric of the land creates a forensic botanical signature, the totality of which imprints traces of both the identity and the abundance of the previous land cover. The faint colouration in the skin of the surface layer, the reds, blues, greens, yellows, greys, and innumerable hues that would take days to match to colour-charts, mirrors the shimmering aqueous tints, like a delicate Japanese watercolour. How often have we said, as we watched the changing evening sky, that if someone had painted this on a canvas, they would be accused of exaggeration, of artistic hyperbole? Walking on the moor on evenings like this, our awareness is absorbed into the landscape in a manner that induces an attenuation of the senses. Suddenly aware of Tormentil, you seem to see it everywhere. The resonant cry of the Curlew carries over an enormous distance in the calm summer air: has it always been here? And this golden light that bathes the intricate features of the land, picking out the evidence of occupation and effort left by previous humans, why have I not noticed that before?

At Àsmaigearraidh, between the crofting townships of Gabhsann and Dail, there is an elliptical green smudge on the browns and greys of the moor, indicating to anyone with any awareness at all that this location was previously a home to someone. At some point in history, they disturbed the local drainage and fertilised the surface, but although they lived there for a while, we do not know their family secrets. We know only that they existed, they were here, and they worked the land! Further south, along the coast at An Gioban, near Mealabost, the slanting sunlight of autumn tends to highlight the strange striped furrows of land that were cultivated at a time so long ago that our society no longer recollects, and I often wonder who those people were. Grazing animals produce differing effects upon the area of their occupation, whether transient or permanent, and this too is a contested feature of the landscape, though we are largely unaware of the contest until it infringes upon our own wellbeing. Too much drainage or inappropriate flooding: overgrazing or croft abandonment, the differences sometimes appear to happen by sleight of hand. There is another splash of green verdure further out onto the Common Grazings, at *Tom a' mhile*, but this is a result of the guano liberally spread by the Lesser Black-backed gulls who sit watchfully at a safe distance. Our sheep used to like to graze here, for the green bite was too tempting, but when they came back to the croft, they brought in their droppings an invasive seed that took us years to rid from the soil. Sometimes we damage the land that we love without intention or comprehension.

## The resident(s) of the bog(s)

Even to those who think they have an understanding of the mineralogical and vegetational conformities of the land, there are unexpected mysteries concealed in this terrain. On the front page of the *Stornoway Gazette and West Coast Advertiser* for the week ending 6 June of the year 1964, there appeared a cryptic yet sensational subheading, *'Body found in peat bank'*.[100] The previous Friday, John and Donald MacLeod had literally unearthed a startling find in a peat bog in the corner of the Arnish moor where the side road to the village of Grimsiadair turns off the main road leading from Stornoway to Harris. Twenty-three-year-old John, from the nearby village of Crossbost, had been part of a crew of eight who were cutting peats (for fuel) for Councillor Angus MacLeod of the village of Ranais, when John's peat iron dug through '*a skull with a bonnet attached*' about half a metre deep in the peat. Initially, the body was thought to be that of a woman, partly deduced from the style of clothing and partly due to the small stature, although it was later confirmed to be a man about five feet four and a half inches tall and 20-25 years of age. The police carefully packed the body (described as having bones reduced by the acidic peat to the consistency of rubbery seaweed) into a case of damp moss and flew it to the mainland for examination. A consequent autopsy by Dr Inkster, of the Department of Anatomy at Edinburgh University, resulted in the sensational front-page subheading in the issue of the paper for the week ending 23 January 1965, '*Peat bank body a victim of murder*'.[101] In collaboration with Dr. Fiddes, of the Department of Forensic Medicine at Edinburgh University, it was confirmed that the victim had been killed by a hard blow to the rear of the head.

A letter to the *Gazette* had meanwhile been published that claimed to shed light on the mystery.[72] Local folklore recounted a story of two schoolboys who had gone out to the moor hunting for birds' eggs and had later quarrelled about the division of the rewards of their expedition. One had hit the other in anger with a stone, and on realising that he had killed his friend, had run away to the mainland of Scotland via Tairbeart. He had afterwards gone to sea, and it was only many years later when his ship had docked in Stornoway and he was recognised, that the story came out. He was tried for murder and hanged on Gallows Hill.

At the National Museum of Antiquities of Scotland (as it was called then) the clothes worn by the victim, and the few possessions that he carried, created almost as much interest as the body itself. In a red-and-white striped woollen bag he had carried a double-sided wooden comb, a horn spoon, and two quill pens.[4] There were no shoes or breeches found, and a leather belt was fragmented, all having rotted during their burial in the moor. A well-worn and frequently repaired thigh-length, close-cut jacket, flared below the waist, was fastened by eleven cloth buttons from throat to waist. Ten-inch-deep cuffs in a different fabric had been sewn onto each sleeve over the ragged originals, and there was a roughly sewn patch covering a hole in the left elbow. This was not the jacket of a wealthy individual, and together with the distinctive style of the other clothing that had been preserved - a shirt, undershirt, stockings and bonnet - the indications are that Arnish Man was probably murdered in the early part of the 18th century. His body had been dumped on the moor (a layer of heather lay beneath the corpse) and slowly buried as the mosses accumulated and turned into peat.

In the peatbogs of Scotland,[20] and throughout north-western Europe,[39] there have been hundreds of human bodies discovered in a wide variety of situations and circumstances. Some of those bodies were so well preserved in the anoxic conditions of the peat that initially a modern-day murder had been suspected. Many of the recoveries date from deaths in the medieval or post-medieval periods, but they cover a wide span of history, for instance a body found in a Shetland bog has been radiocarbon dated to 1490-1655 CE,[20] while mummified remains from Cladh Hallan, in South Uist, are thought to be Bronze Age (2200-700 BC).[83] The apparent motivations for these burials are equally diverse, ranging from murder to symbolic ritual sacrifice, to simple accident. In terms of landscape, it is important to remember that environments change, and the location where a body is now found is most likely to be entirely different from the original situation where it met its fate. Combining multiple aspects of the context of those internments, using pollen analysis, invertebrate remains, and the hydrological history obtained from coring samples, new research has attempted to understand the reasons for the geographical positioning of those bodies within the landscape. Superficially, it is easy to imagine that such landscapes represent remote, uninhabited, confusing, and dangerous places, neither wholly land nor water, liminal spaces at the edge of contemporary society. Even among many of those people who sought out these peatland domains, whether as hunters, transhumance pastoralists in their seasonal shielings, or simply as travellers, the *deep* knowledge of what the landscape contains has seldom been well known nor fully understood. We rarely know the exact historical configuration of the landscape, but we do know that it has not always looked, extended, or occupied the boundaries of geography or of the habitats that are currently apparent.[16] Significantly, the term *àirigh*, the seasonal territory of the pastoral practices of the crofting counties, referred not to the buildings out on the moor, but to the land itself, (the accommodation was a *both*, the root of the word *bothy*) and many of these abandoned and ruinous places are now being rediscovered.[86]

## TERRITORIES AND TESTIMONIALS

There is no doubt about it, the world looks an unfamiliar place when viewed from ground level. I am sprawled-back in a field of knee-deep grass, waiting for a Corncrake male to appear from a damp hollow below me containing a patch of Yellow Iris. The terrain is perfect for Corncrakes, but this is the first time that one has been in this particular spot for seventeen years, and I don't want to miss it. Waiting was easy at first, almost soporific, the ground was dry and sweet-smelling, but now I can feel the moisture seeping into my drawers and I think I might have permanently lost the use of my legs. Just at the moment that I am about to crack and give up, a Meadow Pipit lands on the top of a fence post barely two metres away from me, and then another on the next post, and another on a third. I hardly dare to blink. Their dark, needle-sharp beaks seem impossibly fragile when contrasted against the pale sky. On my other side, a Wheatear flutters in to perch on the top wire of the same fence, so close that I can see the detail of the white tail feathers like a delicate fluff. The four birds bob on their perches for what seems like endless minutes, and just when I decide to move, a Curlew glides into the long grass fifty metres below me and vanishes. I'm tempted to raise myself on an elbow and try for a photograph, but I know that it is too soon. If I move, the Meadow Pipits will flee, and they will alert the Curlew. Even amidst the long grass of the hayfield, I am exposed from above, to the hyper-analytical eyes of a Greater Black-backed Gull which floats on an air current about seven metres directly above me, checking, presumably, that I am alive; and instinctively I fidget to confirm that I am. With supreme effort, I try to ignore an annoying black fly that hums persistently around my eyes and nose, because I know that if I move suddenly, I will give my position away. Eventually all the birds leave me, the Curlew soonest of all, and fighting the stiffness in my limbs, I decide to call it a night. As I'm climbing up the brae, the Corncrake calls again, from exactly where I thought he was hiding, mocking me. Across the river, a Curlew (the same one?) sends its pristine cry into the evening sky, and I wonder (not for the first time) how many other animals are within the scope of my view in this landscape but not apparent to my sight.

Admittedly, if we really would like to understand the invisible (to us, at least), but sharply defined territorial barriers on this open moorland, then looking at the niche habitats of birds is probably a good place to start. When most humans look across hundreds of hectares of unfenced peatland, we tend to see only the unimpeded horizons. Walking across this terrain, however, as you must do in order for your stories to retain any credibility at all back in the pub, would reveal a very different reality.

The creatures that share this terrain with us have no such concerns, and know that all these unmarked territories are intimately connected in a seamless, multi-purpose landscape.

Sometimes, with the wind blowing onshore, the smell of the seaweed tangle is so fresh you can almost taste it in the air. No lover of coastal habitats could ever mistake the immediacy of that tang. Rafts of 'seagulls' bob in the relatively calm eddy behind the surf that trundles onto the ancient, re-worked shingle. How incredibly reductionist is that terminology, simply to group them all as 'seagulls'? There are fierce -eyed Herring Gulls, massive Greater Black-backed gulls, the far-travelled Lesser Black-backed Gulls, Common Gulls (actually, less common here), possibly a vagrant Icelandic or Glaucous Gull, and at the edge of the cluster, like nervously expectant younger cousins, nimble, darting Black-headed Gulls, almost petite in comparison, hoping to glean benefits by association but not wanting to attract too much attention to themselves. Further inland, it is a different scenario.

At the edges of the village, a gull colony is re-occupied afresh each spring, and with the gulls returning to inhabit their portion of this landscape, the Bonxies (Great Skuas) also reappear, and their relatives, the Arctic Skua. I use the Bonxie as a very deliberative example, for although gulls are attentive in their aerial displays to defend the territory that they claim as their own, they are mere amateurs in comparison with the Bonxie. Watch a Bonxie for a day or two and you can begin to understand the idea of an invisible mosaic of bird territories covering this landscape. The territories jostle together, overlying each other in an interactive network of fiefdoms, some of which are mutually compatible, and others of which are in deadly competition. On a flattish expanse of moor close to where I live, I performed a simple experiment. About a hundred and fifty metres away, on the top of a dry tussock that rises no more than half a metre above the surrounding land, but enough to give that little extra height to scope a wider view of the landscape, sits the solid, dark brown shape of a resident Bonxie. As I walk directly towards the bird, s/he (who spotted my presence long before I saw it) rises skyward on spread wings. I stop at once and reverse my steps. The bird settles down again. I walk fifty metres or so to my left, keeping my distance from it, then walk forwards once more; the bird rises again. I repeat the process from every direction, moving clockwise around the position of the sitting bird. Each time I cross that invisible boundary I get a similar response, and the patch of ground defined by the polygon within which the Bonxie is prompted to rise, most definitely marks the limits of its 'comfort zone'. I know from similar previous surveys that if I go any closer to the nest, I will be met with increasingly robust aerial challenges, beginning with a brusque flypast, and graduating to hostile speedy approaches around the height of my waist. The gulls will wheel overhead and screech in intimidation, swooping low for effect, but the Bonxies will target your head and will make direct contact. Getting a solid thud from a Bonxie of perhaps one-and-a-half kilograms, flying at you with a violent rush of air, is enough to make even experienced surveyors flinch, and the lower you duck, the more you can be sure that their next charge will be even lower. As soon as you retreat outwith the extent of *its* territory, (for there is no doubt who has the upper hand), the bird will settle on the ground. There are no markings on the ground to delimit the boundaries, but you now understand the meaning of 'territory'. From this defended zone, the Bonxie will make sallies to various other parts, to raid for eggs and nestlings, to force passing birds to drop their prey and then snatch it up before it hits the ground, but always circling around to return to base. Discovering the remains of a young Greylag Goose or a Meadow Pipit may be the only visible evidence of life interactions that were - and largely continue to be - undetected by human perception.[40]

Around the physical map of this place there are countless other territories recognised by dozens of other species, all equally invisible to us, but nonetheless real. A tiny ball of feathers that we call a Skylark loudly asserts its presence by a repetitious but erratic song, high above us. Their game of find-me-if-you-can can test both your eyesight and your sense of direction, with their inordinately loud ventriloquism seeming to come from everywhere and nowhere specific, until finally (if you are lucky) you spot a tiny dark dot, away, *way* up there. You might think that it was a random discovery, but the next time you walk past that exact spot, it will happen again. I can punctuate the route of some of my walks by the regular Jack-in-the-box appearance of Skylarks singing precisely above their self-defined territories.

A Redshank, although not territorially possessive, may return to the same tuft of grass and the same bare nest-site scrape in the earth, year after year.[46] Curlews are possibly my favourite, however, combining their longevity (a lifespan of possibly 20-30 years) with their remarkable fidelity to place. A bird normally returns each year to forage and nest in the same corner of the same field, or the same hollow on the wide moor, that they did last year and the year before. Only those who have already made the considerable investments of time and energy can hope to fully appreciate the tantalisation, the frustration, and the extent of patience involved in managing to get close views of Curlews without unduly disturbing them. From 300 metres away, they will see you approaching and decide to take a temporary leave of absence. They are more cunning than the Bonxie, or perhaps just less accepting of confrontation, for the spot where you see them take to the air is probably a short, furtive walk away from their nest, successfully distracting you from the latter. Likewise, their soft, slow, long glides into a landing only allow the briefest second to get a fix on them with your lens, for the Curlew will immediately zigzag through the tall vegetation, remaining largely undetected, and will be swallowed up by the land. If you wait, the bird might reappear, but fifty or sixty metres from where you last saw it, so unexpected, in fact, that for a few seconds you might assume that it is a different Curlew.

I have always been suspicious when people talk about a 'spiritual attraction' for that often seems to me to be a loose, ill-considered notion to avoid investigating the real factors that trigger the deeper connections with a place.[54] I am certainly not saying that the scientific engagement with an ecosystem provides the only answers to the question of what 'makes a place special' but dressing it up in vague quasi-religious mysticism doesn't help. Sitting in the margin of a hayfield, with the other local inhabitants of that place largely accepting my presence, I can at least begin to understand our ancestors' attraction to animism and their relationships with 'sacred' places. Would they have called this place *uiseagach*, (a place abounding in Skylarks) or *guilbneachag* (a place of Curlews)? I don't know, but I would like to think so.

# 4
# Under the skin

EMPATHY WITH A PLACE CAN BE HARD TO
DESCRIBE, BUT YOU MAY KNOW THAT FEELING.

Until I was halfway through primary school, I really didn't
understand the difference between somewhere and nowhere. I
believed, in fact, that Nowhere was an actual, identifiable
place. This misunderstanding arose because I had been
told, by several reliable people, that Cailean had come from
nowhere. In one respect, that is true, because it seems like he
just appeared among us; one day he simply turned up, and

almost before we knew it, the impression was created that he had always been here. I can remember my father talking to me, sitting at the end of the byre while he was sharpening a scythe, and telling me that he remembered seeing Cailean walking steadily down the horizon of our moor on that first day. He only possessed what he carried on his back, and that wasn't very much, and he needed work. He wasn't *looking* for work, but he needed some way to pay for something to eat. Fortunately for him, it was the shearing day in our township, and though nobody could afford to hire an extra hand for money, his assistance was welcomed, and he was a good worker, so he shared our food when the time came. I believe it was Domhnull Mòr who took him home and fed him at the end of the day. Big Donald had done a fair bit of rough travelling himself, when he was younger, and he recognised the situation, so now that he was living alone he enjoyed hearing the stories of the younger man. Cailean was given a place to sleep in the barn, and I dare say that it was just as comfortable as being in the house, for Domhnull Mòr kept everything spotlessly in its proper place.

His given name was Colin, but everybody called him Cailean (kalan), for though the poor man arrived with no Gaelic he was more naturally thought of by us as a Cailean rather than a Colin; and anyway, he soon picked up the rudiments of conversational Gaelic, for he was a wonderfully quick learner. Some said that he had come from Aberdeenshire, and others identified somewhere near Galloway, but Cailean always somehow managed to avoid confirming anywhere in particular. So, when my mother said that he came from nowhere, it made perfect sense to me that it must be a village in the lowlands somewhere. Although he was a stranger, he was more like ourselves than any other stranger that I had so far met.

He was very softly spoken, very polite, with sparkling, vivid blue eyes. I remember his eyes in particular, for they seemed to be alert to everything, and even to read your unspoken thoughts if you were not careful. There is no doubt that he was a well-educated man, *very* well-educated, for though he was never verbose, nor loudly opinionated, he could converse effortlessly on seemingly every topic and any place. Some of the men who had been in the army, or the merchant navy, would mention a location, casually testing him, and yes, he had been there once, and could convincingly talk with them about streets and the bars, although you were left with the impression that he could equally easily have chatted about what he had seen there in the galleries and libraries. Domhnull Mòr began to notice small things, a loose fence fixed, a drain unblocked, nothing that you could take offence at, but useful things. Soon, Cailean would occasionally be sought out to give a hand with bigger projects, like moving the sheep to clean pasture, repairing a fence, or levelling a peat road, and he accomplished it all with the same respectful competence.

I now suspect that he would have moved on to somewhere else before the winter arrived, had he not become captivated with my big sister, Catriona. In the way of those things, it was my mother who first spotted it (she has always had an empathy with diverse sorts of people and their relationships, no matter how much they try to hide or deny them). It began with leisurely walks around the township on a summer's evening, after whatever work of the day was over. We all did it, so I was blithely unaware at first when my mother urged me (with that particular tone she reserved for something that was not just a random suggestion) to accompany Catriona and Cailean on their strolls. We would casually meet, as if by accident, at the gate leading to the fank, which was the favourite rendezvous because the paths cross there that lead to the shore, or the moor, or simply make circuits of the village, depending on where your fancy took you.

We began to walk almost every evening over that summer, and into the autumn, and in retrospect I can honestly say that is where and when my education in natural history began. Cailean would pluck a tiny stem from the vegetation, or point out a distinctive flower, and proceed to tell us their names (for he had more than a few words in several languages) and elaborate with interesting information about the lifestyle of that plant. We would sometimes get down on our hands and knees, our noses at moss level, trying to isolate and name all the dozens of individual plant species in a square of land no bigger than my giant childhood pace. I still identify more botanical oddities by their scientific Latin names than I know them by their Gaelic or English equivalents, and that I owe to Cailean. 'Everything is hitched to everything else', he would say, which I thought was a magnificently original phrase until I learned with surprise many years later that it is actually a direct quotation from the pioneering ecologist, John Muir. Cailean said that he saw a richness in this land, and it took me many years of study before I knew for certain that he was correct.

By the time November had arrived, Cailean had moved out of

the barn and into a spare bedroom of Domhnull Mòr. The two men shared an easy camaraderie. I would now take sprigs of plant life to Cailean for identification, and Domhnull Mòr would sometimes chip in with strange background stories that this flower could be boiled and drunk cold to cure indigestion, or that one used to be taken as a remedy for headaches. His stories were patchy and often muddled, but they suggested a treasure chest of lost wisdom and mysterious traditions that I later retold in school. Miss Gillies was a young teacher, just out of probation, with enough enthusiasm and unorthodoxy to fan the embers of my interests. On a couple of occasions she took my scraps of vegetation and turned them into a class lesson. It was a slim reward, but my obsession with so-called 'weeds' acquired a grudging level of legitimacy among my classmates, and I was subsequently directed to an Aladdin's Cave of books in the school library, which fuelled my studies further. In that exotic world, no big game hunter could have diminished my stature.

When the golden light of spring evenings returned, even I could not fail to appreciate that there was a developing connection between Cailean and my sister. They had a sort of telepathy which flowed between them, swerving around me and above me but never including me, although curiously never completely excluding me either. With the open acceptance of a child, I suppose I assumed (if indeed I thought about it at all) that we would go on that way forever. The cyclical changes in the land, the seasonal progression of colours and sounds, the return of land management tasks, had a natural and comfortable familiarity.

Before the shearing time came around again, Cailean and Catriona were married, and he had moved into our house. (With her consummate practicality, my mother had decided that they were a perfect match for each other, so why defer their happiness any longer?) I had mixed feelings about this arrangement, I must admit, for though I was now able to spend more time in Cailean's company, I also had to share him with my sister (and acknowledge that there was a part of him that was off limits to me). The trade-off for me was that we had moved beyond simple botany, and Cailean had now introduced me to geology, and the geomorphology of the land, and the complexities of bird behaviour (in as much detail as a ten-year-old could reasonably absorb). With a rapidity that mesmerised me, Catriona became pregnant and grew steadily in girth. For as long as she was able, they continued with their walks every evening, slowly, and progressively shorter in duration as her pregnancy advanced. Even over the winter months, they would snatch a quick stroll together before the full darkness, if the weather was not uncomfortable. They would sometimes choose the path along the coast, and the next evening do the circuit route of the crofts, a different aspect of the village landscape each day, as if gathering the experiences together to savour during her confinement.

It was one of the late spring days after Easter, when I came home from school, and I knew at once that something was wrong. There was an unnatural hush about the house that often seems to accompany a life-changing personal crisis. There was no sign of my mother, which was very unusual because she gently dominated the house, even in her temporary absence. There was no sign of anyone, actually, although I could hear my father in the distance, shouting at the cattle. Initially I took little notice, I was decompressing from the day in a classroom and finding my own space again. As the silence in the house extended, I understood that all was not well. I figured that my father was probably moving the cattle to the top field, the place that we call *Cùl na clachan*, literally 'behind the stones' because it lies along the farthest boundary of our croft, where the thousands of stones were dumped when they were cleared from the fields in a first attempt to improve them for agriculture. I wandered in that direction, thinking perhaps that others in the family might also be with him.

My father was a good man, industrious, painfully honest, but not the most communicative of individuals, so the story of the day emerged disjointedly, sporadically, and with a great reluctance to embellish. Basically, my sister had gone to move the cattle from one field to fresher pasture, an activity that we had both done for as long as either of us can remember. Normally this is a gentle stroll, the cows take their time, ambling at their own pace, stopping to tear a mouthful of grass after every few steps as if they have been starved for a month. Whatever happened, and we still don't know, something spooked one of the cows and it jumped, banging into my sister, and knocking her to the ground. Here my father was even less coherent, but I got the gist; lots of blood, fears for the baby, and the dash with my mother and Cailean to the hospital twenty miles away in town.

The rest of my afternoon was a bit of a daze. In fact, the rest of the day unravelled in staccato scenes of unreality. When eventually my mother and Cailean returned, they brought the news that neither Catriona nor the baby had survived. There had been complications. I wanted to scream, "What can be so complicated!" but instead we were all dumbstruck. When we talked at all it was in apologetic hesitancy, about mechanical things that needed to be done. There was no joy, no spontaneity, only fumbling attempts to come to some understanding of how this tragedy could have visited us.

I won't describe the aftermath, for we all have to deal with bereavement in our own ways, to cope as best as we can, and for most of us the details are highly personal and don't really benefit from debate. Cailean remained with us for barely three more months before he told us that he had to go. I tried to suggest to him that he could simply move to town. He would still be a part of our family and we could visit each other as often as we wanted without encroaching on our private spaces, but he made it clear that this was not an option for him. "This place gets under your skin," he told me at one point. "Once you have experienced it, *really* experienced it, nothing else will suffice."

"Then don't leave," I begged him, but he explained in simple, eloquent sentences that in this landscape, on every path and from the corner of every field, every view was irrevocably embedded with memories of Catriona, and those lost possibilities were draining the life from him. He needed to leave and lose himself in… somewhere. A place so completely different that the pain would be disconnected. Perhaps he would go back to the desert, or perhaps try Alaska, he had never been there yet.

He left at the height of summer, when our nights refuse to get completely dark, and the wild birds call to each other all the time in the serenity of that abundance. We said our goodbyes, but we didn't see him leave, taking only what he could carry. On the kitchen table he left me one of his books on natural science, inscribed inside the front cover, 'To Dr Colin _____ with affection'. Underneath, in his own handwriting, he left a short message for me, and it is no maudlin hyperbole to say that the gift of that book changed my life. It was the germ of my future career and my portal to the deep ecology of this landscape where I was born, live, work, and will very probably die, although hopefully not too soon. Intermittently, over the years, a postcard has arrived for me from some unexpected location, and I have puzzled long and hard over the cryptically brief messages. I have read since about the historical phenomenon of the 'scholar gypsy': that person (usually a man) who is highly educated but chooses to drop out of society and 'go native' at the most basic level of engagement with the land that he can tolerate. That, I now realise, is the style of Cailean. The postcards have become less frequent in recent years, but I still look forward to receiving another reminder one day, and I imagine him travelling, out there. Somewhere.

# 5
# Layers of meanings

Surely, the classic representation of place, however basic, is a map. Any map, even a rough, out-of-scale sketch map. Or is it? In any form of analysis, maps tend to tell us not so much what we know, or want to know, about a place, but how much the cartographers are prepared to tell us. Any map is merely a pictorial representation of what were considered (at the time of preparation) to be the most important geographical landmarks. The 'importance' of those features changes with time, with the purpose that the map is used for, and with the political significance that those features have acquired.[9] Even a hill that has remained in the same locality for millennia may suddenly become an impassable boundary between 'us' and 'them', a landform to be captured, defended, or ignored, depending upon political leanings. In common with many other languages of the world, in Gaelic/Gàidhlig, the indigenous language of the Gàidhealtachd in the Highlands and Islands of Scotland, the names of specific locations on the map denote their functionality and appearance. The use of colour terms provides favourite adjectives, as do descriptions that highlight an association with the native fauna or flora, and of course the recognisable shape of the landforms - big, small, rounded, flat, sharp, and so on. The language describes the land, and the land enriches the lexicon of the language, not simply in the description of topographical form or colour, but also in the rich terminology of all the varied provisions of the land, including water, fuel, food, and aesthetic benefits - what is called in modern parlance 'ecosystem services'.[67]

In terms of colour, in the small area surrounding my own village alone, there are listed among the two hundred or so placenames *Blàr glas* (the grey field), *Geodha ruadh* (the red sea-gully), and numerous other gullies, black, white, blue, and so on, *Lèana bhàin* (the white/light-coloured swampy meadow/ plain), *An gàrradh dubh* (the black dyke) and many more shades in the surrounding landscape. So far, so good. Or is it really that simple? On the one hand, the naming conventions in Gaelic enable a native speaker to navigate through the landscape with little prior knowledge other than a list of the place names likely to be encountered. Physical appearances are important. There are many subtle differentiations in the size and geomorphology of hills; for example, *sgorr* is a pointed pinnacle, *meall* is a rounded hill (smaller than a beinn - mountain), *cnoc* is a hillock, and *tom* is a mere uprising of the land, not even distinctive enough to be considered a *cnoc*. *Beinn dearg* is a red-coloured mountain, *Tom buidhe* is a yellow hillock, keep the former feature on your left side and the latter on your right hand and you will be straight on track for your intended destination. A great many of the place names are graphically descriptive of the shape of the landform, or the colouration produced by the natural vegetation or by the underlying geology. *Dearg* is often an indication of red granite, or perhaps the occurrence of an injection of pink pegmatite, *geal* (white) may suggest quartzite, while *dubh* (black) is frequently basaltic, or applied to lowering cliffs and gloomy gorges. On the other hand (and this is significant), colours in Gaelic are much more contextual than they are in Standard English, and as we will see later in this book, the description of a particular chromatic colour in Gaelic is heavily dependent on the landscape setting, rather than simply the frequency of the absorbed light. The implied meaning of a colour in Gaelic can change to represent a range of shades that might be lumped together as one word in Standard English. This might be considered confusing, unless you actually live amongst these changing colours, watching them as the seasonal light is diffused across the land. It is an intricate texture of cultural nuances that entertains as well as informs.

## WHAT'S IN A NAME?

Some people have asked me occasionally, why does it matter that we should try to understand the naming of the landscape features that we live amongst? Depending on the preceding conversation, I have usually tried to reply in terms of historical perspectives, or by identifying the personal attachments associated with a particular place, but that only partially explains it, because we sometimes call the same place by different names at different times in history, and even according to our different moods. Let me try a different analogy. Let's think about the various names that we give to the people that we know in our own life - sometimes simultaneously referencing them with completely separate nomenclature.

For a start, there is the Scottish custom of a woman adopting the surname of her husband when they get married. So, for example, Anna MacLeod becomes Anna MacDonald. She is still the same person, but now we have referenced her slightly differently. In more recent times, a woman may decide to retain her original surname, but that does not mean that she is not married; her social situation has changed but not the name that she is known by. Frequently women, especially in the academic world, choose to retain their original surname because it helps, for example, to maintain a continuous record of their publications, rather than trying to build a professional reputation again from a blank start. They may also choose to use their married name in other contexts of their (non-academic) life. Sometimes they may decide to combine the names in a double-barrelled surname, and although that

79

may create a little confusion with successive generations, there are ways around that too. There are changes that may occur with divorce. Does the person keep their married name or revert to their original family name? In a couple of cases that I am aware of, my friends have adopted a third option, which is to take up the family name of their mother, because they no longer feel comfortable with the earlier two previous options. They seem to feel, in some way, that they have become a different person.

Nor does this renaming and reconfirming of identity only affect women. In many (most?) cases it is also culturally conditioned. In Iceland, the cultural naming convention is to adopt the suffix, ...sson or ...dottir to complete the first name of your parent. So, Magnus, the son of Edvard, will be Magnus Edvardsson, but if Magnus has a son, also called Magnus, he will be named Magnus Magnusson. In a small, close society, this is intimately relatable, but in a larger, more metropolitan community, it may be harder to follow someone's lineage, although their gender is immediately identifiable.

I have a good friend in Bhutan who has only one name, (although he has two fathers, as two brothers married the same woman simultaneously). It is unclear (to us) if this single name is a first name or a surname (when he travels abroad, he simply states the name twice as he has discovered that the international bureaucracy of immigration officials usually demands a first and second name to be registered for each individual traveller!). Although I have known him for nearly two decades, I only recently discovered that the name that he is known by (to everybody), is not his given name at birth. As a child he showed particular educational promise and was given the opportunity to take up a place at a good school that had already been promised to a village friend of his (the friend by this time had acquired another offer in a different school). By agreement, my friend simply took the name of the child that he was replacing and retained that name for the rest of his life. (He occasionally meets his namesake, who is still a friend).

As I was growing up, my introduction to naming the land that surrounded me was by learning (almost by osmosis) the Gaelic names of the hills and the rivers, valleys, shorelines, and peatlands that I was walking across. That awareness illuminates and frequently helps to explain the details of landscape when you can understand the language employed in the naming. To offer another social comparison, there are at least five simultaneous ways to name a person in the Gaelic language.

- There is their name in Gaelic, e.g., Iain Mac a' Ghobhainn

- Their same name in the English language - John Smith (Some people may have their birth name registered 'officially' in English, yet never be called by that name).

- Their patronymic name, i.e., who do they come from? e.g., Iain Mac a' Ghobha, Mhic Alasdair, Mhic Domhnaill Ruaidh (John, son of the Smith, son of Alexander, son of Donald the red - probably referring to the reddish complexion or ginger hair of Iain's great-grandfather).

- Then there is also the possibility of a nickname, or a descriptive name, because there may well be several persons of this same name in the school class or in the village. So, the person might also be named Iain Mòr (Big John) or perhaps some obscure nickname given by his friends in jest because of his appearance, or his hobby, or his similarity to a contemporary celebrity.

- Lastly, there may be a pet-name, or familiar name, that is most commonly used to identify the person. So, Domhnall (Donald) might get called Dan, in a similar way to the English name, Elizabeth, being rendered as Liz, or Lizzie, Betty, or Beth.

It is not at all uncommon for the relations, friends, and neighbours of a person to alternate between ALL these different names, depending upon to whom they are speaking, and in what context. (Even the wife or sister of John Smith may never refer to him by anything other than his nickname or familiar name, and rarely, if ever, by the name registered on his birth certificate!) All these names refer to the same person, but they may reflect a context in our relationships with that person, or the level of our intimacy with them, or simply the bond of familiarity (or not) that we share.

In the same way, we each inherit an affinity with the land and the landscape of our own habituated environment. Whether our ancestors have been living there for many generations, or whether we have relocated geographically and have only lived there for a very short time, we are *all* dependent, to a greater or lesser extent, on the land. It might only be that we walk around the locality, or that we own/rent the land that our house is built upon, but even the most tenuous link is unavoidable. We exist. We walk upon this earth. Whether we choose to acknowledge the extent of our links is another matter. I have written in other places,[87] about such locations as An Gearasdan. The original name for the place was Inbhir Lochaidh (Inverlochy), the mouth of the River Lochy, but in the Hanoverian pacification of the Highlands and Islands it became a strategic point of defence and was re-named Fort William. To the Gaels who inhabited that place, it now became known as *An Gearasdan* - The Garrison. The place where the soldiers are - beware! Three names for the same locality, each sensibly descriptive, but each conveying such very different meanings. These multiple layers of naming and topographical understanding abound throughout our landscape, if we care to scrutinise the terrain.

As I have also tried to explain,[89] an in-depth exploration of place, or an immersive experience with the landscape that surrounds us in every direction, will be slightly (or hugely) different for each one of us, and those experiences will condition both the depth and the cultural positioning of our own understanding. A friend of mine, who has moved to the island to settle, told me recently about the walks that he enjoys in the vicinity of his home. He included a mention of the beautiful 'Bay of Pigs' just along the coast, which seems incongruous, until you are aware that the 'pigs' were in fact *muc-mhara* - 'sea-pigs' - whales - which given the high sea-view from the headland site makes complete sense. These layers of meaning that are applied to the land are sometimes transparent, like the oddly named Mol Èire - twice-named, for this means 'shingle beach' in the two historical languages of the place - or the 'Eas mòr waterfall' (the big waterfall waterfall). The name might also be suggested by the landform's colour or shape. Sometimes successive cultures replace and re-name places, sometimes they simply adopt, adapt, and absorb. Each appellation has an individual history, just like two people from the same family.

The collective agglomeration of those understandings by the whole community, the recognition and fixation of subsequently identifiable places, is part of what we call 'culture'. Although cultural values change, morph, diverge, and become rediscovered, the basis of that collective awareness remains as a framework, a lattice against which we measure our perceptions and our perceptiveness as a society.[97] The land, whether from the environmental, social, economic, historical, or political perspective, is the source and the foundation of all those nuances of geographical recognition. The names that we give to the places in the landscape, no matter whether it relates to their physical shape, their colour, their functional use, or their historical or spiritual legacy, are the foundations of our awareness of who we are and how we come to be precisely here, in this named place. That is why an appreciation of the naming of the landscape is so crucially important.[36 and 37]

## Quantum landscapes

After writing articles about 'the other landscape' and how places can apparently be imbued with characteristics and features that are visible to some people but hidden completely from others, I have received quite a few emails. Fortunately, none of them supposed that I had been talking about supernatural attributes (perhaps they know me too well) but I was surprised how deeply the concept seemed to resonate in the wider readership.[95] Several people genuinely wanted to explore in greater detail this idea of how we might come to appreciate, and possibly explain, what we might mean by 'a sense of place'. Above all, there is a fascination with the concept that the landscape might be a complex, overlapping array of sensations, appearances, and attributes that vary from place to place, and from person to person. That set of variations will change, both for the individual observer through time and between different observers, so the concept might seem to be a will-o-the-wisp. Often, it appears, we each understand the same place very differently, and at least part of the human quest for 'meaning' in life is to grasp that elusive insight and to comprehend it as fully as we are enabled to in that specific moment of time.

What I am going to write next might bring some enlightenment, or it may simply confuse the issue further. What it certainly will *not* do is to help you to understand quantum physics (in as much as anyone ever really understands it). Nor is it advisable to take the comparison too literally - it's really only an analogy, hopefully a useful one. The following is a suggestion for an alternative way of thinking about 'the other landscape' that I hope might offer greater clarity (but take it lightly, don't get sucked into pseudoscience).

When we look at a landscape, or immerse ourselves deeply in a place, we see it as a certain observed reality.[104] There are many ways in which we can measure or describe that appearance of reality. Some obvious factors that could be employed are the physical parameters, the latitude, longitude and altitude of the place, its humidity, climate, and air quality. Then, expanding the idea of place beyond a single footprint of land to encompass an entire section of landscape, we might add a consideration of the aspect (the direction it faces - sunward or shade?) as well as the complete hydrological system, the soil types, the covering vegetation, and the habitats that they provide for the various species of fauna and flora in that place. We might ponder the different influences of atmospheric conditions of the place (weather) and the climate (the effects of weather over a long period of time). Then, of course, there are the impacts that the human species has made on that place, both the physical imposition of changes (roads, farms, drainage, buildings)[103] and the intangible aspects of society and culture (legends, stories, songs, old images, names on a map and other heritage examples).[99] There is the terrain (the surface features of the landscape spreading out before us) and then there is the terrane (the geologist's three-dimensional block of Earth that extends a place below the superficialities of the surface to include the millennia of rock strata) that quite literally supports the world we walk upon.

All these multifarious factors contribute to the creation of a place, and of course they all change over time. Here is the quantum comparison though, because this perceived reality not only is different for every person looking at that place, it is also different for each individual every single time we look at the place. Although some changes may be invisible (the subterranean flow of water, for example) other differences only become known slowly (learning a historical anecdote connected to a piece of land) or remain forever hidden from our deepest awareness (like the nocturnal movements of an otter or the unfailing navigational attachment of migrating birds). All these different realities of place are real, but the reality is unique to different people and different times simultaneously. Like Schrödinger's cat, which quantum theory indicates can be both dead and alive at the same time, the quantum landscape is both the same (in memory, at least) and intrinsically different every time we perceive that place. It is apparently changeless and at the same time constantly changing.

To make sense of this paradox we can adopt the realisation of quantum mechanics, that multiple realities coexist (indeed, multiple universes) or we can simplify (as many physicists do) and try just to understand more deeply, more completely, the singular reality that we personally perceive, feel, smell, touch, and enjoy at any one moment. Avoiding the wormhole of postmodernism that seems to deny any objectivity in anything, we humans have the advantages of being able to communicate in networks (that we call communities) and we are able to share and agglomerate our knowledge, and even our subjectivities. This facilitates multiple interpretations and empathies with the perceived reality of a place, what a place can mean. We can attempt to express that sense of place through writing, arts, photography, film, or utilitarian social activities. Or we can simply enjoy the quantum variations of place - the differences between the static fluctuations and the (de)localisation of the observable. As a Buddhist practitioner will strive to do, we can try to be fully in the present.

# 6
# The meaning of life?

ATTACHMENT TO A PLACE MAY NOT BE ALL
THAT IT APPEARS AT FIRST.

It was the stark brutality of his sentence that shocked me.
I come across a lot of different types of people in my job,
and basically, they are usually just ordinary people in diverse
combinations of life circumstances. They usually have a lot
of money, I mean they need to be reasonably well off before
they can afford the prices of the estate, but usually they are
pretty decent in the way they treat you. Often, it's the ones that

you don't expect to be nice that you end up getting on well with. Perhaps there *is* a distinction between the people who have made their own money, and the ones who have been left a bundle by mummy and daddy. I don't know. Anyway, I was really taken aback when he first said it to me. He sounded very bitter, and …. as if he was talking about an animal, not a man who was sitting right beside him, hearing every word that he spoke.

The first time that it happened, we were just back onshore. I was pulling the boat up on the small sandy beach in Loch an Eòin while he was admiring the sky, hands on his hips, not bothering to help me.

"What a sky! It reminds me of the clear evenings in the desert of Arizona. Have you ever been to Arizona, Angus?"

"No, indeed."

He stood back and looked at me, with his head tilted as if he couldn't believe his ears. Apparently, everyone has been to Arizona.

"What about Canada?"

"No, well…."

He didn't give me any time to explain all the various ports that I had been in, and something in his demeanour prompted me to take the piss a little bit.

"I believe that I was in Glasgow once and …," I began, but I got no further.

"Paris? Rome? Have you ever been to the Far East, or Australia?"

I wondered where this monologue was going, so I decided to say nothing.

"The joys of travel broaden the mind and make the man." he said to me, almost like one of those old-fashioned preachers. Then, I'll never forget the look of complete disdain on his face. He stood back and looked straight down his nose at me (I had never realised until then that some people can actually do that) and said, "You are stuck here on this remote little island, and you have seen nothing. Absolutely nothing! What a waste of a life!"

That really stung, but with that, he turned and strolled off back to the Land Rover, leaving me to carry all of the shooting gear and the lifebelts. I didn't know whether to shout after him in anger, or just to ignore it. To tell the truth I was a little confused at what had just happened. Did he really believe that I had never left this island in all my 50-plus years? I was going to say something, but I didn't know where to start so as not to make a big deal out of it. I decided that I didn't want to give him the satisfaction of a response. In the event, it was settled for me, because he turned his face to the side-window and ignored me all the way back to the Lodge. I tried to start some light conversation, but he didn't respond, so I just drove home and pondered on what Joan might have made for my dinner. As my mother would have said, (her most vituperative comment), "A thoroughly unpleasant man".

The following morning, it was as if nothing had happened. Two of his friends from London had come up to join the party, and he obviously wanted to impress them with how well integrated he was, so it was "Angus this" and "Angus that" and "Do you think, Angus, that...?" It didn't impress me, and I don't know what it did for his friends, but they were chatty and we had a pleasant enough day, although it was ruined at the end by one of his friends poking his head above the heather just as he was going to shoot. The stags, of course, were off before he could even count them, and we then had a long, wet, empty-handed walk back to the Land Rover.

The following day was much the same, and the day after. At the end of the week his friends returned home, so it was just the two of us out on the hill, and he seemed to be in another of his disgruntled moods. He started on me as soon as we got into the Land Rover.

"What's it to be today then, Angus? Valparaiso?... Montevideo?"

I didn't let on that, actually, these were places that I could tell him plenty about, and I wondered if he had ever been there himself. Nor did I want to have to justify myself about where I had been or what I had done. I have never felt that I am 'remote' by living in the island. I left to travel when I wanted to, and I came home when I wanted to. Being 'away' has always been more of a period of comparison, rather than an 'escape' for me. How could I possibly convey to him anything about the years that I had spent working the mines and the sheep ranches in Australia and New Zealand? Or about the feelings, eventually, that brought me home? There is a great joy in travelling, but an even greater satisfaction in coming home to a place where you truly belong. Would he even understand the sense of place that links islanders to their native soil and rock, no matter in what bright corner of the globe they end up? The Gaels have a word for it. We call it *cianalas* - I guess the loose translation is 'homesickness', but that is a very weak comparison. People have been known to die from *cianalas,* just wither away in a corner and give up on life. In the days before Skype and international mobile phone calls, migration to work in the forests of Canada or the tea plantations of Assam meant little chance of ever seeing your relations or your home turf again. For an islander, when the adrenaline-fuelled joys of adventure wore out, and the ennui of *cianalas* set in, there were only two choices – return to your roots or look out your shroud. One day, I looked out across a series of incredibly beautiful ridge lines, grading deep green to fainter and more washed-out shades as they stepped towards the horizon, and I was suddenly reminded of a particular view of the Hebrides. I was in Wanaka, New Zealand when the *cianalas* got to me, and I was on the next plane home.

I had got all that out of my system long ago. I have been around the globe several times and now I know where I want to spend the rest of my life.

It was when I was driving down the road to the old pier, musing on these thoughts, that I realised that he was speaking to me again. At least, he was speaking aloud, intending that someone should hear, and I was the only other person in the vehicle.

"... and do you never miss the opera? It's the opera and the big-league games that really *make* London for me... and the concerts of course, have you never been to the Royal Albert Hall…?"

I stifled a reply to ask if he had the ability to distinguish the difference between a pibroch and a port-a-beul, but I knew that the question would be wasted. Then he said it again, as I was turning down the top of the old slipway. He said, as if he was considering just to himself, but loud enough for him to know that I had no alternative except to hear it.

"Such a waste of a life."

I felt my cheeks burning again, and there was such an almost-visceral reaction that passed through me that I had to prevent myself grabbing him by the throat and asking what the hell he meant by that, but the moment passed, and I dispersed my energy by getting the gear out of the back of the Land Rover.

"I think I would like to go over there today," he said, indicating Little Brebhig island with a general waving of his forefinger.

"I was planning the rough corrie," I replied, indicating the opposite direction entirely.

"No. I want to go over to the little island today!"

"Well, there's not really much chance of a trophy there."

"I don't care, it's part of your beat, isn't it? Well, I would like to go over there, even if I don't get a shot at any decent beast. It's the new experience that counts, eh?"

I shrugged. It was nothing to me if he wanted an easy day. We might get the chance of a useful shot at a scraggy, broken-antlered stag, but the walking would certainly be

much easier, and it was no bother to me if we saw nothing
but rabbits and terns all day. I loaded the gear into the dinghy,
and when it was stowed, I set the outboard towards the long,
golden sands of Little Brebhig, instead of skirting around the
headland to come around to the other side of the mountain.

The strait between the 'mainland' of Lewis and Little Brebhig
is not wide, scarcely more than a couple of hundred metres,
but the long-shore current is fierce. We needed to steer in a
broad curve in order to hit the small island. It's not *really*
dangerous, but there can be spectacular white turbulence on
the surface of the sea when the tide is in full flood. I tossed him
a lifejacket, as normal, and when he didn't pick it up to slip it
on, I cautioned him.

"Life is about chances," he said, "You balance the risks and
take your chances, that's what you people need to learn. It's not
that far."

I had neither the time nor the inclination to debate with him.
Handling the tiller can be quite a struggle when you first
get out beyond the shelter of the headland, and I needed to
concentrate on keeping the boat steady. He sat in the stern,
looking back at the shore as if he owned it and not saying
another word to me until we landed on the beach of Little
Brebhig.

The rest of the day was uneventful. There were no deer on the
island, (as I knew) but even if there had been, he showed no
inclination to pick up a gun. He wandered around - along the
strand, up the dunes, there seemed no pattern to his movement.
At first, I started to point out features of interest - the site

of an old corn-drying kiln (and probably an illicit still), the markings of the old cottage walls where generations had lived, and the remains of the turf dyke surrounding the village - but he made it clear that he didn't care to listen to me and slouched away. I followed him at a little distance, still unsure what he wanted to do, but after an hour or so, he turned sharply on me.

"Do you *have* to follow me like a little dog? I just want some peace. I'll see you back at the boat!"

I bit my tongue and walked back to the beach. We are always told that the paying guest has the say on how far and where they want to walk - so long as it is safe and legal. I went back to the boat and began to tidy some gear. What did it matter to me if he wanted to pay stalking rates just for a walk along the shore?

He was gone for quite some time. Normally I would have been a bit apprehensive about leaving a client alone, but it was a very small island, a lovely sunny day - warm even - and I knew that he couldn't get lost. After a while I simply lay back on the dunes, watching the birds dive in the offshore shallows for sand-eels. Even so, I was quite glad when I saw him picking his way through the heather back towards the beach.

The walking tour of Little Brebhig hadn't improved his humour. It was long past lunchtime and I offered him something from the hamper, but nothing I had satisfied him. He wanted to return to the Lodge. Right away! I was a bit reluctant to leave, not because of the short day, but the tidal current was still going strong, and if we waited a wee bit longer it would be a more pleasant trip back to the Land Rover. But waiting wasn't on his agenda. I explained about the long-shore current, but he was working himself into a mood.

"That's your trouble," he hurled, "always looking for the easy life! You live in this remote corner of the planet, a beautiful place where nothing ever happens, and yet you still want life to be easier. You waste your time doing nothing, going nowhere, risking no excitement!"

I nearly asked him how exciting it would be to him to receive a burst lip, but all of a sudden, I was tired of him. Tired of his selfish moods and his snide comments. It would be a pleasure to take him back early to the Lodge and get him off my hands. Today was his last full day, there would be no time tomorrow to do any stalking. I threw the gear into the bottom of the boat and started to slide her back into the water.

We were going fine until we were about half-way across, then a big lump of water caught us side-on. Sometimes the shape of the seafloor creates awkward swirls and big holes in the surface of the ocean, and we practically fell into one now. I saw it coming, so I was able to steer her round-and-out without too much trouble, but when we popped out of the hole another big lump of water hit us. I don't know if he was frightened or if he was just showing off, but suddenly he stood up and started shouting directions to me. I yelled at him not to be so bloody stupid and to sit down, but the next wave was upon us again. With the boat rocking and him waving about, I couldn't hold her steady, and as neat as a pancake she flipped over. I was in the water before I really knew what was happening, and I knew that with this rip current I had to swim strongly for the shore.

It was only fifty metres away, but in those waters, it might as well have been five hundred.

As I kicked for the rocks, I could see his head being swept away to the south on a torrent of foam. There was no way that he could reach the beach now. Across the zinging of the water-rush I could hear him yelling, although it took me a few seconds to distinguish his words. Then I heard him clearly in a silent lull of the tide.

"Help me!" he called, "I can't swim!"

I could hardly help myself, there was nothing else that I could do or say. As I caught a calmer stretch of water and struck for the nearest shore I shouted back to him, gulping water as I did so.

"Never learned .... to swim? ... What ... a waste .... of a life!"

I kicked for the shore, knowing that I would need to get home immediately and report the accident.

# 7
# The layers of belonging

## ROOTS AND BRANCHES

The layers of nuances of our belonging to the land are the
most intricate, the most convoluted, and the most emotional.
We are invested, almost without our consent, in the history
formed by the stories that we have received from our
ancestors.[96] There are times, moments of discovery, when
we 'come upon ourselves' (as Neil Gunn would say)[45] and
we recognise some intimate relationship between ourselves
and someplace special, other times we are left confused and

perhaps disturbed by the polar mismatch between the given interpretations and our own understanding of the world.

All around us there are layers of habitation, in time and in space. When I arrive in a landscape that is different from my own natural habitat (which, let's face it, is almost every other place) I automatically devour the details with my eyes and begin to decode it. Looking at a new landscape is similar to opening a new book or viewing a new painting in a gallery; the words, the images, are recognisable, but I need to take time to process the story of what they collectively reveal. I first might see the glacial sculpting, rounding, and scouring the topography, then the notches subsequently cut by running water, the thickening texture of trees at various stages of growth, different combinations of bird species, and the scatterings of broken scree like some grey Cyrillic writing against the patchwork greens of opportunistic grasses and mosses. The chapter of this story is unfamiliar, but I know that, with time and effort, I can learn to reassemble the blocks of knowledge and learn to read the language of this new terrain.

The language of 'belongingness' also changes, however, as do the nature and the depth of the connections. It is not simply a question of scale, but also of perspective and of cultural roots. One million of anything seems to be a huge number, but one million seconds is equal to just over eleven-and-a-half days, and even after one million seconds, my view of the land can be substantially different. Contemplating the changes that have occurred over thousands of millions of years of geological time is an exercise to stretch the most creative imagination. Partly, it might depend as much upon physical orientation as upon mental proclivities. Arriving in this village by boat, after a rumbustious sea crossing, will set a totally different tone of expectation than will be obtained after a day-long bog-slog over one of the largest intact blanket bogs in Europe. Both views of the welcoming greenness of the shallow glen, cleaving the crofting land in two, will be well received by the traveller, but perhaps for different reasons, and those will condition the mental images, and the cognitive maps. The 180-degree contrast in line-of-sight, whether facing the ocean or with your back to the ocean, is only a small part of the difference. A panorama will reveal the same natural features, and human experience might make similar connections, but the whole sense of place may be radically imprinted by those earliest impressions. What you actually see will be influenced by whether you are primarily a hunter, a pastoralist, a farmer, a land speculator, or a tourist. (Of course, each individual may view the place with multiple roles, and this can create its own tensions and variations in perception). Recently, a Babylonian clay tablet, used around 3,700 years ago, was re-examined in an attempt to decipher the symbols scratched on its surface and it was concluded that it is a record of the oldest-known example of applied geometry. The small clay tablet, labelled (precisely, if somewhat unimaginatively) Si.427, was found to employ 'Pythagorean calculations' measuring triangles 1,000 years before Pythagoras was born, to register the exact details of a Mesopotamian land deal. Land was important, then as now, and the scribes needed to provide carefully-collected evidence to clearly understand what land was being discussed, in order to avoid any future disagreements between the seller and the buyer.[69]

Obviously, those views of the land seen from the water will be partially formed by the purpose(s) of the voyage. An arriving peripatetic cleric of the church of St Columba will have had a particular mindset and denominational aspirations that would bear no commonality with a passenger on board the vessels *Metagama* or *Marloch* as they left the land behind them on their sail to establish a new life across the Atlantic.[108] The horizon and the superficial impressions would have been comparable, but the emotional relationships must have been quite different.

Out of the blue, one morning, I received an email notification from Chris Fleet with a link to the new LiDAR maps that are now held online by the National Library of Scotland. LiDAR (Light and Detection Ranging, sometimes called 3D Laser scanning), which are basically high-resolution 3D images created by bouncing laser beams from space and analysing the reflections, can be used to create incredibly-detailed maps of terrain. When I clicked on the link and studied the area of my own village, the effect was almost overwhelming. Unlike conventional paper (or other digital) maps, the laser technology *sees* into the land. In addition to the clear delineation of the roads or contemporary houses, the new lidar map reveals the rickles of stone foundations buried in the ground, the roots of the pre-clearance village, and other skeleton structures that date back beyond human memory.

Shadows of disrupted historical drainage and rock walls outline structures that are not readily visible on the ground, even when you are standing right on top of them. In this one image there are four, if not five, separate layers of civilisation spread out for our scrutiny. For a moment I nearly wept. Stretched across this map was the evidence, now hidden from view, of a vibrant culture that had flourished where I now sit, two hundred years, two thousand years, before today. It feels like looking at a historical crime scene.

If any confirmation is required that different civilisations look upon the landscape with contrasting perspectives, this is it. The four main episodes of settlement in this locality, the current, the recent historical (up until the middle of the nineteenth century), the Iron Age, and the Mesolithic, lie in overlapping vectors of orientation across this terrain. Between the gaps in these epochs of settled habitation are displayed the sketchy remnants of human occupation that are so old and fragmentary that even the tenuous but persistent legacy of Gaelic communal memory has no clear recollection. Nevertheless, the remnants are here, visible during a few brief glances in the slanting light of the low winter sun, or captured for perpetuity on the satellite lidar maps by the penetrating laser light that searches out every bump, hollow, and shadow of the terrain. I have read that lidar scans have been used in South America to identify lost settlements hidden beneath the canopy of the rainforest, and I wonder aloud what remains to be discerned on the environmentally and culturally bared landscape of the Gàidhealtachd.

# ATTITUDES

In the final analysis, a great many people are able to see only what they want to see in the landscape. The chances are that if you want to escape to wild spaces, then emptiness will be what you will find. A diametrically-opposed psychology seems to find only challenges; nothing that you travel to discover is as good as the things that you left behind. The middle ground (no pun intended) is much more difficult to negotiate. Humans talk about 'improving' the land, usually meaning changing it from the naturally-occurring ecosystem to something more economically profitable, for example agriculture or forestry. Rarely is the land valued for what it actually is. Even 'wild land' (although in the vast majority of cases that epithet could be seriously contested) is often seen as being beneficial only for its 'recreational value' as if its sole purpose for being there is to entertain us. In terms of the UK, and for most of the mainland of Western Europe, there is no true 'wilderness' remaining,[14] and though extensive areas of land may have various levels of legal designations to protect their integrity as a 'cultural landscape'.[92] or to maintain their ecological biodiversity, the governing bodies have been slow to realise that what is really required is a whole-countryside approach to the management of natural ecosystems.[24] In many areas this reality remains unacknowledged by the people who have the power to effect the serious and genuine restoration of the natural ecological systems of the land.

My father once told me that he didn't know *any* shepherds who went hillwalking simply for fun. As an enthusiastic

hillwalker, that brought me up short and made me think. Our
attitudes towards the land are never simple or straightforward,
no matter how close to it or distant we might imagine ourselves
to be. A perceptive analysis of the changing attitudes toward
the appearance of the land has been presented in the historical
context of the Highlands and Islands of Scotland.[98] It traces
the evolution in thought from viewing the landscape as a
fearsome, untamed, unbounded *terra incognita*, through
the phases of discovery and familiarity, to its contemporary
image as a recreational refuge and 'lung of the city' that is
both prevalent and pejorative in the modern discourse. The
argument for 'rewilding' is frequently deliberately loose and
ambiguous because it often chases after a mythical vision of
the past that is not resilient under close scrutiny. It ranges from
a cogent vision for the reconstitution of a countryside-wide
functional natural ecosystem (which I would wholeheartedly
support) to the creation of a mystical ecological past at some
random, unspecified and unsubstantiated date, (of which I
despair). Key characteristics of entrenched attitudes are that
we are often unaware of where we acquired them, and that
we rarely feel that we need to justify them with any logical
comparison with reality.

My colleague, the historian Elizabeth Ritchie, in a short but
astute academic analysis of current perceptions of 'wild land'
in the Scottish Highlands and Islands, noted that,

> *'The decision to name parts as 'wild' is merely
> the latest manifestation of a longstanding set
> of attitudes that romanticise the Highlands*

105

> *by exaggerating the extent to which the area is*
> *untouched by humans'*[91]

despite the evidence that this landscape is not absent of the
impacts of a historically resident population. In fact,

> *'You can zoom in to where people lived before the*
> *deliberate depopulation of inland areas between*
> *c.1770 and the 1850s. On the ground, the sinuous*
> *mounds of soil for oats, barley and kale, and*
> *the dykes built to keep out the livestock, are still*
> *visible.'(ibid)*

In many of these locations, the Gaelic terminology of the
landscape is all that remains on most maps to indicate that
people lived there, were familiar with every aspect of the place,
and utilised the terrain productively. The name *Badcall* of the
crofting township in Sutherland, means *'the place of Hazel
trees'* in Gaelic, but now Hazel have grown there for many
generations. In a similar manner to the naming of natural
features of the world, the historical Gaels have applied their
skills of parsing the land to the human ecology of subsistence
farming and agricultural survival.[23] Although, to the passing
town-dweller or tourist, the scenes may appear identical, it was
important for the resident ruralist to be able to differentiate
between *deisear* (a place having a southern exposure) and
*tuathair* (countryside with a northern exposure). Similarly,
there is a world of difference between *sonann* (fertile land) and
*spad-thalamh* (unproductive fallow ground), or *aitheornach*

(land ploughed for a second crop) and *ath-thodhar* (land remaining untilled for two years). Proximity with the land engendered subtle but significant distinctions that identify the positioning of landscape, the *ceann-mhàg* (the head ridge in a ploughed field) versus the *corr-fhòd* (the concluding furrow) as well as whether the ground is *sgribhinn* (the rugged side of a hill) or *morbhach* (liable to flooding by the sea). There are numerous terms specific to the productivity of the landscape, whether the terrain is *dail-bhuntàta* (a potato field), or *coirceach* (abounding in oats) or *eòrnach* (barley land) or *ingealtas* (ground fit for feeding cattle) or *laomach* (a piece of land where the corn falls flat from exuberant growth). There are various descriptions of the size, configuration, and productivity of meadows and grazing land, and of course only a fool would fail to understand the difference between *claigeann* (the best field of arable land on a farm) and *daibhir* (the worst pasture of a farm). As Elizabeth Ritchie highlights, the human perceptions of the landscape are often not straightforward, and,

> '*The irony for those who feel that more human activity necessarily means a greater threat is that greater human presence in the past created a more productive and diverse environment than what we are striving to protect today.*'[91]

For these reasons, 're-peopling' the countryside has become a valued mantra, and the term 'ecological restoration' is being championed above the term 'rewilding'. These are not just pedantic terminological distinctions, for when the survival of yourself and your family is dependent on the ratio of what you might produce from the land in comparison with the collective effort that is required to secure it, the awareness of those differences might mean penury or comfort. It is a measure of the distance that profligate society has travelled, from the farm to the city, that Standard English has largely dispensed with this necessary understanding. The ability to *read* the land, to see the potential and the problems, the ease and the effort required, is so much more than simply appreciating the scenic view of the countryside. For people who live *on* the land, *by* the land, *in* the land, the descriptive naming of specific places is not simply a fad, or an affectation, which is why it is worth getting to understand traditional place names, and why it is (perhaps unintentionally) so dismissive to ignore or rename these locations with modern indulgences.

## Belongingness

In an island (albeit the largest island in the archipelago of the United Kingdom), where virtually every small village has its own bard (poet), Lewis is not short of songs and poetry, prose, and praise, that express the full range of human connections with the land. As with every other genre and culture, the verses can be wonderful or woeful, and often the richness of the idiom is lost in translation, rendering the original poignant sentiments into maudlin English, but the best compositions can be heart-stopping. One of my very favourites is not a song of exile, but the reflections of a serviceman in the Second World War, Malcolm MacLean (Calum Beag Chalum Iain Aonghais), from the village of Tabost, in Nis, written at the end of his leave in 1940.

## Deireadh leave 1940

(Verses 1 and 5)[19]

*O, Leòdhais mo ghràidh, dèan innse dhomh 'n dràst'*
*An àm dhomh bhith fàgail do ghlinn,*
*'N teid mi thairis air sàl 'n dùil tilleadh gu bràth*
*No an slàn le mo Thàbost a chaoidh?*

*Gach cnoc agus beann, gach struthan is allt,*
*Gach gleann tha'n eilean mo ghaoil,*
*Ma's nì e nach till, 's nach bi mise leibh,*
*O, 's math bhios mo chuimhn' air gach aon.*

Oh, Lewis my love, tell me now
At the time of leaving your glens,
Will I go over the ocean with hope of ever returning
Or is this farewell forever to Tabost?

Every hillock and ben, every stream and river,
Every glen in my beloved island,
If I am not to return and will never be with you,
Great will be my memories of each of you.

Fortunately, he did survive that war, but I never listen to that song without becoming a little emotional. It is easy for me to imagine the thoughts that went through the poet's head as he prepared to leave his home and return to the theatre of a global war that appeared to have no resolution. Fond images and memories of home, and the intimacy of connections with a favourite place are common to many people, of course, even if these were accentuated by the trauma of a war in progress. What may be less frequently acknowledged is the depth of this connectivity. In Gaelic there is a word, *buntanas*, which, broadly translated, embraces the concept of *belongingness*. This is not simply belonging. It is a pervasive universe of associations that extend beyond where you live, where you are from, beyond the network of family and community contacts, to include a comfortable, self-defining embeddedness that reinforces your place as a connected component in the world. You are not isolated, (though you may choose to favour and emphasise particular associations) and you are not defined by the concept, but it loosely describes the totality of the milieu that you inhabit.

There will be many people who are familiar with the sensation of pleasure or relief that they experience when they are returning home after a long journey, when they get the first glimpse of that recognisable hill, or road junction, or river crossing, that signals that they are almost home. In some people, and I consider myself one of this clan, this connectedness to landscape is attenuated to a much finer degree. There are parts of my immersive landscape locally that I almost feel related to as a family member: I know the

place names, and I have watched them and walked them in all
seasons and all weathers for almost all of my adult life, so I
feel that I have an inside track on their changing events. There
is delight when new, deep sand suddenly appears in a place
along the shore that was previously only rocks and shingle (and
corresponding regret when the sea removes it all for recycling).
There is a shiver of pain when discovering a 'blow-out' on
the machair that exposes the vulnerable roots of the land,
literally clearing the way for the coarse ablation and removal
of the land surface. When I was in my early teens I used to play
with my friends in a certain favourite glen among the hills,
semi-feral in the long summer days. I have not been back there
for years, but I could take you tomorrow to an obscure cave in
the middle of that glen, hidden from all but the most diligent
of searchers. It is a small opening, probably hewn at some
long-forgotten period in human history in a futile attempt
to find precious metals, for there is a small shaft sunk a few
metres along the tunnel. The name of this structure is Rankin
Rennie's Cave, and I used to take a proprietorial delight that it
had once been used as a dwelling by a namesake of mine, who
had distilled illegal whisky there and had tricked the gaugers
when they raided him one day. It is not only the picturesque
views on the surface of the landscape that lay a claim on our
emotions, but sometimes even the half-lit recesses, deep in the
bowels of the geological terrane, although I very much doubt if
there are still one hundred people alive who know the location
of that cave, and fewer than ten who know its name.

These emotional nodes in the landscape are to some degree
familiar to many people. The sensation that now is often

described as a 'sense of place' was regarded in classical times as being caused by the spirits that inhabited those places, the *genius loci*, and it was assumed that those guardian divinities infused the place with their good or bad vibes. On six continents I have visited 'sacred sites' by which it is meant, I think, locations that have a special relevance in the culture and worldview of that indigenous community. The classical description has now become '*the genius of a place*', that is to say the particular combinations of the natural environment and the cultural connotations of the place that resonate with a certain section of human society. I have to say 'I think' because, although I might be able to empathise with the physical influences of that place, the associations with any deeper religious significance are lost on me. A friend once wrote to me and asked why I did not write about the religious elements that describe a sense of place in the landscape, and I replied quite honestly, that it was because I did not want to move into the realms of hypocrisy. If by the term 'spiritual' you mean the inner realisations of an individual, then I can relate to your philosophising, but when you attempt to attribute the marvellous workings of the natural universe to a quasi-mystical sequence of supernatural manipulations, then we have to part company. For me, the infinitely interconnected cause-and-effect of rational chemistry and physics, the behavioural psychology of species, and our complex interaction with the natural world, hold a great deal more fascination and marvel than the nebulous persuasions of blind faith. When I sit on the horizon of my world and look downhill, across the wide Gabhsann moor towards the western ocean, I hope that I can be tolerated for thinking that the sounds of the natural world are unequivocally more attractive.

Undoubtedly there are physical locations that have a powerfully-rooted resonance for certain people and can unmask our innermost feelings. I remember one anecdote of a good friend, a piper, who busked his way around Europe as a student, playing the bagpipes whenever his funds began to get low. In a beer garden in rural Germany, he began playing to facilitate contributions that might enable another round of drinks, and after the first tune a local drinker at a nearby table turned as white as a sheet and dashed away. Later, as he collected the coins, the local's friend sidled up to apologise. "You need to understand", he said, "the last time that my friend heard that music he was at El Alamein in the smoke of the desert war, and that sound is associated with certain memories for him".

At a more mundane level, there are the melodies embedded in the land itself. How many people are aware that the apparently monotonous (and repetitive) call of that iconic bird of traditional farming landscapes, the Corncrake, is singularly distinctive of each individual bird? Each *crex crex* syllable of its rasping call, when analysed using auditory science, is sufficiently distinctive to be able to identify the individual birds (it is only the males that broadcast their presence, in the hope of attracting a female bird). The two apparently-identical syllables can in fact be measured to show that the duration of each syllable, the silence between syllables, and the space between each pair of syllables, is, within a very large sample, unique to each individual male. With care, the analytical technique can be used to say that the bird calling in *this* field last night is the same one as in *that* field over there tonight. In a dwindling and regionally-threatened population, the ability to place individuals that move around the landscape between breeding attempts is potentially vitally important for its habitat management and survival.

Nor should we confine our appreciation of the music of place to the natural sounds of the animal kingdom. In 1829, Mendelssohn visited the island of Staffa on his tour of Scotland, and his subsequent *Hebrides Overture* was evoked by the sensations that vigorously stimulated his imagination. Among the singers and musicians of my acquaintance, there are several (I fear to risk my friendships by isolating the specific few to illustrate the substantive point) who epitomise the melodies of *buntanas*. My friend, the late Ishbel MacAskill, could effortlessly still a noisy room with the perfect clarity of her voice and her emotive tone, as can the similar talent of Julie Fowlis, who can send shivers up many a spine when she sings about her Hebridean landscape. The fiddler, Duncan Chisholm, inspired so many people with his daily tunes on social media during the pandemic of lockdown, that the beaches of Sandwood Bay, and the route 'far over Struie' have become beacons of hope and connectivity with a favoured place among the firmament in the shifting unreality of this age. In my particular wallow of traditional Scottish fiddle music, I am unashamedly in awe of the ability of Allan Henderson to render with infinite precision the landscape of a Gaelic air into music that leaves me bedazzled. As he plays, I can almost hear an invisible figure behind me, whispering the words of the tune that he hangs on the air, and pervades the landscape with its visceral notes. This is so much more than simply pleasant music, it is the connecting thread to *buntanas* that produces a collective awareness of belonging, and a spiritual reciprocity which takes the inducted listener beyond mere kinship and geographical co-location, beyond Middle Eastern folklore and the vagaries of history, to a glimpse of the landscape that is moulded into personality.

# 8

# The white house

CHANGE IS INEVITABLE, AND OFTEN
UNPREDICTABLE.

The building simply sat in the middle of the village like a
toothless gap in an otherwise healthy mouth. The eye of any
observer was inexorably drawn towards the lowest point on the
single road through the township, so that it eventually focussed
upon the four black windows and the slightly squint roof with
the lean-to on one side. Peter would often sit on the stones at
the corner where the two dykes met, especially on Sundays or

on the long, calm, summer evenings after a day's work. From there he had a complete view of Brebhig, from the seashore to the moor, all the houses, of every family, on both sides of the burn running through the middle of the village, but still his eye was drawn to the white house.

His sister, Mairead, was still a little bit afraid of its empty, staring, windows, even though she was eighteen and nearly ready to go off to university. They had all been a little frightened of it when they were younger, for in their earliest memories there had never been anyone living within its walls. A couple of years ago an English family moved into the house, well, it was just a shell, to be honest, solidly built, but with the air of an aging celebrity past their prime but still holding on to the spotlight. The couple had one young child, a baby really, and the woman's old mother who was frail and partially blind. There was a scepticism in the village that they would stay for long, but most people were quite glad that there was a light in the window at nights. Through the long twilit evenings of summer, they watched the new family clean the windows and paint the inside of the house. They didn't get around to tidying up the garden, but the folk of Brebhig weren't much on gardening anyway. A few less charitable mouths inevitably said, "We'll see if they last the first winter", and sadly their suspicions were proven right. With the arrival of early gales, clattering the ridge tiles of the roof, and the rain consequently being driven in at the loose-fitting windows, they made a miserable time of it. When the real winds started in March, they didn't even wait for the brighter months of the Spring lambs or the return of the migrant birds and the glorious long

117

days of summer. One day they were in Brebhig, the next they were gone. Some said they had only gone as far as Stornoway, but news filtered back, as it always does, and confirmed that they had left the island for parts unknown. The house was empty again.

As a child, Peter remembered the stories he had been told of the clearances, and in his fanciful young head (for although it was only three generations ago, he had never been taught a single sentence about the Brebhig clearances in school), he imagined the white house as a legacy from those evictions. It was a convenient fallacy and for a while it served a purpose. For a time, when he grew older, they had played in the ruined outhouse that used to be the byre to the croft, and once, when the wind had burst a windowpane and allowed them entry to the croft-house itself, they had explored the silent rooms like a foreign country. Only once though, for the damp smell of the air and the scurrying of rats held no more than momentary fascinations. Some men came then, from Stornoway he was told, and boarded up the broken window, so they could no longer get inside, even if they had wanted to. Yet he felt the house contained something which belonged to him. It was part of the village as much as he was himself a part, and it held a fascination of unknown histories within its walls.

The house was unusual for other reasons, for it didn't really belong to anyone, though of course it did, technically, have an owner. It was the only house in the village which was not actually on a croft. Many years before, when the white house had contained a vibrant family, the children had gone off one by one to jobs on the mainland, returning for holidays, but never with any eye to permanence. The youngest son, Angus, had felt compelled to follow his brother into the merchant navy. In time the brother, and his sister, died in the war, and after his mother's funeral Angus had decided to dispense with the house without returning ever again to the island. His future was being planned for elsewhere. He separated the house from the croft land which surrounded it and gave the croft over to his remaining younger cousin. The house was made available through a lawyer in Stornoway, and in this innocent way he sealed the death of the house (there was no Airbnb in those days, for good or for ill), for though there was a chain of prospective buyers, none of them lasted any distance. The years had passed since then.

When Peter returned from university, he would sit at the corner of the dykes and watch the younger children of the village playing boisterously along the quiet road. Though he would listen to the stories of the older people around an evening fire, and hear their complaints that the village was dying, he knew in his heart that this was not true. The bigger families of the old folks' youth would certainly have populated the township more effectively and completely than the standard 'two children, one of each' of his own generation, but he knew enough of history to imagine a life of hardship and subsistence agriculture and compared it with his own full life. There was a pride under his skin, as yet unarticulated, which drew his attention to the social life of the village, to the young people who were staying on, and he knew that the majority were living in Brebhig through choice, not from a necessity brought about through the lack of any alternatives. Over that second summer

119

holiday away from his studies, he came to realise that the inevitability of his return to Brebhig, at some misty point in the future, was perhaps the most solid fact of his own existence.

From the corner of the dyke, he knew that the sites of three dùns could be seen, although the towers themselves (whatever functions they once fulfilled in the history of this place) were now no more than scattered piles of tumbled-down stones among the encroaching Deergrass. A few hundred metres on either side of those dùns were the remains of three entirely different cultural civilisations, reluctantly emerging from the layers of vegetation. There were the Norse incomers on the Sand Park, and before them the Iron Age and early Mesolithic settlers hugging the shore, and even before them the nameless explorers who have left the marks of their agricultural attempts scratched on the land at Torsuigabac, but little else by which to remember them. The geography of this village, should he choose to draw a map, would be as clearly demarcated to him as the lines of drainage *feithean* on the moor, or the lines of white Gannets against the blue sea, or the dark brown, almost black, delineations of newly cut family peat banks. Behind several of the modern houses stood the previous generation of old blackhouses, with their thick, double layers of dry-stone walls and their rounded corners to shed the wind. Most of those blackhouses now presented gaping holes to the sky, where once a cosy thatched roof had covered a family and their cattle, but a few of the buildings had been maintained and converted into outhouses for crofting tools and bric-à-brac. The blackhouses, he learned, were not called by this name until the white houses (built with cement) arrived to present an architectural contrast. Looked at from this angle, the seamless continuity of the people who had belonged to this place was simply a long, colourful, and intriguing narrative. History was all around him, and the current inhabitants were plainly just another chapter in the progress.

Another half a dozen years were to pass before this realisation re-surfaced, however, and after a regular return visit home, sitting on the same dyke, he wished more than anything that he didn't have to catch that ferry on Monday morning. There is a Gaelic word for it, *buntanas*- I suppose that 'belongingness' is the nearest word in the English language. It doesn't just mean where you come from, it's deeper than that. It is who your people are, your connections in the community, your whole heritage, your … *rootedness*. You don't need to study *buntanas*, it just grows on you, a slow awakening, (if we were in one of the Asian countries, we might call it 'enlightenment'), and with this gradually emerging realisation came a change in Peter's lifestyle. The pace of his work altered, not slower, as might be imagined, but faster, to accommodate his preparations to return, to find job opportunities at home, and yet still keep pace with his normal employment. When the time came to move, the release of emotion was like a downpour on the moor. The turbulent flow of his life tumbled white-frothed, bubbling, and coloured brown with the peaty earth of his own place. Walking on the high road that weekend, he knew that this was still not enough. On Monday he went into Stornoway to speak to the estate agent.

From the high point of the road as it heads north along the coast, the dip of the land immediately draws your eye to the solid white house in the centre of the village, with its cluster of freshly painted outbuildings and dark roofs. The view from the front window gives a magnificent view straight down the shallow V of the glen formed by the village river, the whole township is spread out for display, and conversely, the white house has itself become a focal point. At night, the light above the door proclaims its presence in the darkness and signals a welcome. There was never any doubt but that Peter had come home to stay, and even the laughter of the children that you can sometimes hear through an open window as you walk along the village road is but a faint, fragmentary echo of the merriment those old walls saw on that first New Year that the white house celebrated its re-occupancy.

# 9
# Layers of perception

## THE SOUNDS OF PLACE

Some sounds permeate the landscape as if they are seamlessly embedded in the fabric of the place. I have been thinking a lot, recently, about the specific soundscapes of the landscape that define and describe special places, particularly island places. In these considerations I am spoiled for choice. Despite, or perhaps because of, the open spaces surrounding my normal place of habitation, and the relative absence of traffic, there is a soft, never-ending backdrop of distinctive sounds that, if they do not actually identify individual localities, can certainly intimately evoke specific landscapes. Fundamentally, there are the two continual acoustic backgrounds of the wind and the ocean. Both can be either gentle on the ear or downright threatening, but they are ever present. Both of these elemental sources of sound have an almost infinite repertoire to present to us, depending upon the changing directions and strengths of the winds and the currents (often, indeed, harmonising in combination). The wind may murmur or roar, but for the most part, to the native, it becomes as natural and omnipresent as your own breath. (You rarely stop to listen to your own breath during the course of a normal day). Of course, the constant movement of the ocean has its own panoply of sound effects: the throaty, intermittent rumble of the surf, the grating of gravelly shingle in the drag of the backwash, (especially during a frosty evening) and even the deceptively playful splashing of wave-tops on the rocks. There is a perpetual background susurration in the broad multidirectional waves, but the ocean lacks the infinite acoustic creativity of the wind.

All these underlying sounds that I can hear in the landscape around my own patch of turf in Lewis may not be markedly different from what is heard by my colleagues in Shetland or in Orkney, or a thousand other archipelagos, but the noises here are as recognisable to me as the voice of an old friend. I'm sure that there are different dialects of the wind, even from village to village as the currents of air bend around varied landforms and buildings to hone their own particular pitch and tone.

Then, laid upon this insular soundscape are layers upon layers of individual sounds which, taken all together, constitute a unique sonic signature that is pertinent only to that specific place. Yes, it is true, the individual sounds may not be unique, but the precise volume and the combination surely are. They form a four-dimensional orchestral blend that builds repetitive variations on a theme, but is never exactly the same, changing constantly with specific location and time. From my seat on the patio behind the house, sheltered by a few stubborn trees at the bottom of the gentle rise of the land leading up our croft, I filter and try to interpret the sounds that I hear. Frequently, I can even follow the movements of invisible fellow species that cohabit this place with me.

There are several pairs of Curlews at the top of the croft, where the inbye fields abut the coarser vegetation of the heathery Common Grazings. As the year progresses, I listen to the calls of the Curlews change, identifying the mellifluous, fluid calls of display songs at the start of the breeding season, through the intermittent alarm calls or all-clear signals, to the series of repetitive squeaks, the joie de vivre of aerial patrols that they make over successfully-hatched chicks. Sometimes I think that I can distinguish the particular call of an individual Curlew, and I mentally follow its flight path, pondering the reason for its journey. Curlews are especially interesting birds (to me anyway) not the least because they are incredibly faithful to their natal sites and usually return to forage and nest in the same areas of the same fields year after year throughout their two or three decades of life. The birds that I am listening to are likely to be the same individuals that held me entranced by the calls with which they filled this landscape last year. Elsewhere, my walks around the village are punctuated by several localities where diminutive Skylarks noisily mark their territory as I pass by below them: mere dots of chirruping song in the air above. A belligerent Hooded Crow complains grumpily at being disturbed, but it is nothing compared to the cacophony of the irritated colony of Lesser Black-backed gulls who are unsettled by my presence. Their larger, distant relatives, the Greater Black-backed gulls, appear to laugh raucously at me from some prominent viewpoint of the terrain. There are single-note whistles from the resplendent Golden Plovers, and impatient, high-pitched piping from the ever-vigilant Oystercatchers.

Turning a corner of a ridge there might be a nervous, explosive flutter of Rock Doves, or the strident cheep of a sturdy Hebridean Wren LOUDLY asserting ownership of this scrap of territory (I cannot contest this). Or the serrated screeching of Arctic Terns that sets the teeth on edge as they defend their nests. If I'm lucky, during the evenings, in the near constant daylight of summer, I might hear an emblematic Corncrake. I say 'lucky' but considering that a single male might rasp out his double-syllable *crex crex* call between half a million and a million times during a breeding season, I can understand why you might not want to have one nesting right outside your bedroom window. I have a special soft spot for them all the same, and I never fail to snap alert with delight when their curious call permeates the air.[90] At other times I have stood watching a mesmerising display of Gannets fishing just offshore, close enough to witness their gymnastic splashes into the sea but just out of range to hear the satisfying thuds of their plunges on impact. The immediate thrill of being among the clamjamfry of two hundred Greylag or Pink-footed Geese as they rise together to fly to a roosting site, filling the sky with the immense volume of their honking and setting the surrounding air into turbulent vectors by their collective flapping, is enough to set any human heart pumping madly with adrenaline. At night as we sleep, as science is discovering through the recording of nocturnal migrations, the birds continue to move across the land, oblivious to us, their presence undetected by all except by the gentle calls picked up by a strategically placed microphone. Seasonal changes contribute to the variations on a theme, like the summertime hum of bees in the garden or the winter whooshing of the wind around immovable objects.

The land itself gives out a less intrusive, more subtle, orchestration which is nonetheless in harmony with the diversity of island habitats. Below our croft house is a sweet water spring that has been murmuring quietly for more human generations than we can count. It is named after the grandfather of my wife, and although it is seldom visited these days it continues to produce clear water and by its steady presence it contributes to the way in which we partially understand this landscape. At a lower altitude still, I can hear the bubbling conversation of the water in the village river, negotiating its obstacles en route to the ocean, in a medley of water noises: a soft bubbling over a ripple, the crash and splash over a small shelf, and the grateful sigh of the smooth pool that is penned up behind the hulking profile of the boulder beach. Out on the moor, I need to listen very, very attentively in order to detect the mysterious *sotto voce* trickling of the subterranean *còs-shruth* draining the peatland through their hollow, tube-like streams. There are almost 10 kilometres of dry-stone boundary walls dividing the fields in this village alone, what David, one of my crofting neighbours, calls 'the singing walls of Galson', so inhabited are these landscape structures by small nesting birds. Each small sound contributes something that is peculiarly individual to the whole effect.

This intricate mosaic of sound is neither entirely random nor structured systematically; it is the entropy of the natural world in motion. It is an increasing level of randomness that grows more complicated as your awareness increases. Nor is the auditory contribution of the human species completely absent in this island environment of wrap-around sound. There are stereotypical interventions that puncture the stillness of the summer air in the villages: the rhythmic clacketty-clack of a Harris Tweed loom in the Hebrides, the distinctive chugging of a marine engine in the Voes of the northern islands. The obtrusive mechanical hum and whoosh of distant vehicles on the main road, or in the air above, make minimal impact here. These tiny signs of human interaction are not universal, perhaps no longer even frequent occurrences, but when you hear them in their totality, you understand intuitively that you could be nowhere else on Earth. In those circumstances, I have suggested elsewhere,[88] you know for certain that you are *in* the environment of the islands, not simply standing *on* the islands.

The silent spaces in between syllables of sound are important too, serving to emphasise the counterpoint between nothing and something important. We wait for the thoughtful, interrogative pause between the warning call of the sentinel bird and the reassurance of safety, or the heightened anticipation produced by a calm interlude in the middle of a storm. The idiosyncratic sound-pause-sound-pause of every Corncrake call never fails to stimulate delight in wondering when and where the next call will sound. We can only be observers of the patient, silent vigilance of the solitary Grey Heron, or the effortless glide of a huge Sea Eagle hunting high above the shore, or the authoritative sharp bark of a Red Deer hind alerting her extended family. As I write these words, I can hear the awesome sound of a pair of rutting stags on the peatland of Gabhsann, roaring loudly in sexual competition, although they are at least two kilometres distant from me. The Japanese have a special word for the concept that the meaningful gaps between objects or sounds can contribute positively towards the definition of something, even in its apparent absence. They call it 'Ma', and how appropriate is that, considering that it has exactly the same pronunciation as *math*, the Gaelic word for good.

## THE ART OF PLACE

Nor are all those significant 'gaps' confined to the aural sensations. In a short but perceptive essay called *Highland space*,[73] Neil Gunn explored this awareness in relation to art. Of particular note here, was the realisation by Gunn that Sesshū, the fifteenth century Japanese artist and Zen monk, had utilised the contrasts of light and shadow in his splashed ink landscape paintings to create the suggestion of barely-perceptible features of the landscape, even in their actual absence. I was reminded of this by my friend, Murdo MacDonald, as our conversation ranged over the representations of landscape in the paintings of Donald (Domhnull Safety) Smith, the Canadian Group of Seven, and Finnish artists such as Pekka Halonen. (Murdo is an Emeritus Professor of the History of Scottish Art,[62] so my contribution to this 'conversation' was largely in the form of questions!). I have several of 'Safety's' paintings, and though I knew the man, we never discussed art, (to my regret now) but for me his portfolio is inextricably imbued with the DNA of the Isle of Lewis.[60] In a similar manner, the vibrant colours, bold lines, and the use of light in the paintings of the Group of Seven,[81] give the images an appealing freshness that could only be emblematic of that specific form of Canadian landscape, and Halonen's snowscapes have a luminescent quality that draws the eye and invites the viewer into the Finnish landscape in a way that informs us without words where this place is. Each letter of the Gaelic alphabet is represented by a different species of tree, beginning A for *Ailm*, the ancient Gaelic word for Elm, to *Beith* (Birch) through the eighteen characters of the alphabet to U for *Ur*, the Yew tree.[66] In merging deep ecology with detailed linguistics, Murdo MacDonald has linked the Gaelic alphabet not merely with the names of trees, but with the textures of landscape that describe the ecology of place that those species of trees inhabit.[59]

The extraordinary ability of some artists to convey their ideas about a place onto paper (or canvas) with just a few sparsely stroked lines or daubs of colour extends into the production of maps. Many of those maps are works of art in their own right, as well as functioning as navigational aids, but this technique conveys added layers of symbolism to the interpretations of the landscapes. Although a map can be thought of as merely a pictorial representation of what we, in our society, consider to be important landmarks, the names of the places identified can chart their pedigree, and as in the paintings of Sesshū, often as much can be conferred by the features that are absent, as by those that are presented. Maps are generally an intricate combination of science, politics, art, and technological design, and this combination is displayed in many different styles. In a museum in New Zealand I marvelled at a map that used shells and pebbles to depict the distribution of islands, with twigs to indicate the surge of the prevailing ocean currents: a portable navigational tool used by Polynesian sailors to describe the important features of their world. This cognitive map was communicated orally, remembered, and recreated when the necessity arose.

Item 88 in the series (radio, podcast, and book) *A History of the World in 100 Objects*,[63] helps to illustrate this point quite nicely. Careful scrutiny of a map, drawn on a deerskin around 1774, shows, *"…an encounter not just between different worlds, but between different ways of imagining the world."* Covering in rudimentary detail a huge area of what are now the states of Illinois, Indiana, and Michigan, the map was obviously created just before the start of the War of Independence in an attempt to acquire more land from Native Americans. There are a number of fascinating features displayed that give some indications about how the traditional owners viewed that land, geographically, culturally, and functionally. The Native American settlements are marked, as are the important rivers, to enable orientation, but none of the settlements of the European settlers are indicated, despite some of those places being already well-established urban centres. This map is as important for what it omits and overlooks (including the intense spiritual attachment of indigenous people to the land) as for what it purports to document. It illustrates entire communities and their ways of engagement with the land, rather than being a record of personal ownership. Looking at it now, with the clear hindsight of history, there can be little doubt that the colonists and the native people both saw in this map very divergent representations of the same area of land.

This, of course, is inevitable, to a certain extent. Tracing the evolution of the maps of one area, such as the Outer Hebrides of Scotland,[68] it can be appreciated that the changing ways of depicting a place have varied (and no doubt will continue to do so) according to the prevailing political allegiance, technical ability, and intended purpose of the cartographer. To those who saw the map as a document that would help them to control, exploit, or promote the assets of those regions, a map could capture one aspect of reality; to those who were on the receiving end of those changes, a totally incompatible worldview might be manifest. Maps, as illustrations of the landscape, are never value-neutral, and though they may be 'accurate', they are also ways of presenting alternative visions of reality, modifying, annotating, embellishing the terrain in certain styles to emphasise or negate what are considered to be important, irrelevant, or uncomfortable aspects of the land.

Once, when I was doing my doctoral research, I had the privilege of consulting the original geological maps held by the British Geological Survey in Edinburgh. In some cases the margins of those highly technical productions displayed beautiful hand-painted watercolours, annotated by the field geologist to indicate the views that would have been visible and their relationship to the rock structure. In the days before digital cameras and GPS tools, this was the way for field scientists to express their ideas about the landscape that they studied. These images were a creative means of expressing the structure and the fabric of the land in an attempt to understand its formation. I have a fond image of a crusty mapper setting down his hammer and pulling out a brush and miniature paintbox to add another layer of cognition to the ground he was walking over. Murdo MacDonald also drew my attention to the detailed 'visual essays' of geological and botanical processes in the landscape paintings of Horatio McCulloch,[57] and the artistically-inventive cartography of John Bartholomew and his colleagues,[61] that combined functionality with beauty. The published effect was stunning, graphically innovative, and popular. Undoubtedly, there are diverse ways of 'seeing' the terrain, and perception is not always as clear-cut as it might appear to be.[49] The maps by Bartholomew established a reputation for accuracy and powerful visual imagery through the creative use of gradations of colour to suggest three dimensional forms, but colour can also be deceptive. In another discussion, I was directed to the artwork of Malcolm 'Mara' MacDonald, from Lewis who emigrated to Canada, but left some emotive images in his detailed line drawings.

Intriguingly, the ways of expressing colour in the Gaelic language are not necessarily directly translatable to their English language equivalent. There are many examples,[58] but *gorm*, for instance, although normally translated as blue, in fact, in Gaelic, suggests blue-to-green. The word *glas*, although often translated as grey, has a much wider connotation in Gaelic to mean a grey*ish*, less saturated, shade that is defined by the context in which the observer views the object. Colour, in Gaelic, is as much about the properties of a particular place as about the exact hue of the colour spectrum. Murdo goes further, to suggest that '*landscape awareness also seems to be at the heart of understanding Gaelic colour words*',[59] and wonders if a fluency in Gaelic influences the visual perception of the land. It is interesting to speculate whether the fantastic water-lily landscapes that Monet painted towards the end of his life, were actually, at least partially, a result of the cataracts that afflicted him at that period, reflecting the way that he really *saw* the views.[27] Rather than painting an *impression*, did he actually experience the visual sensation in that famous soft, slightly fuzzy, perspective, and accurately paint what he observed? In a similar manner, Murdo speculates whether the visual perception of William McTaggart, as a native Gaelic speaker, influenced the ways in which he depicted colour in his style-breaking landscapes,[32] and led the way for other artists to follow.

There is an interesting concept emerging in the health sciences that is being termed 'palettes of place'. The basic idea is that human beings respond to the preponderance of different colours in the landscape. Most research on this topic has been done on 'green landscapes' and blue, and to a lesser extent on vistas that are predominantly white.[11 and 33] Without oversimplification or taking a dogmatic stance, it seems that these landscape palettes can have a beneficial therapeutic effect for people recovering from a variety of conditions, including physical and mental stress.[29] The predominance of certain natural colours in our environment affects our mood, and this in turn affects our wellbeing. We literally relax into the land. It is tempting to speculate whether we like certain landscape paintings because of a physical-mental reaction, as distinct from a response based upon personal dis/likes or experiences, and cultural conditioning. I have pondered with several friends who are artists if those 'therapeutic paintings', those artistic images that are soft on the eyes and stimulate us to feel good, have been created by the artists because that is the way they saw the landscape, or because it is the way that they felt about what they saw, and mostly my informants agree on the latter. 'It just feels right'!

In a different context of territorial allegiance, Mara was one of the artists who contributed artwork for the authoritative Gaelic-to-English illustrated dictionary compiled by Dwelly,[31] and among his line drawings in that dictionary is a schematic rendering of the *comharraidhean-cluas chaorach*. These are the traditional earmarks for sheep: notches and patterns cut into the ear(s) of each beast to indicate its ownership and the land where it belongs. One look at the ears of a stray ewe gathered at a township fank would be enough to indicate its provenance, and although the practice is rarely used these days, these historical records are like miniature charts reflecting the patterns of belonging and occupation of this land.[18] They are micro-maps that overlap layers of identity, territory, ownership, and tradition. Each of these diverse ways gives recognition to the images of the land outside the back door and may be a valid conceptualisation of place, even though the different images might appear contrasting or even contradictory. In the absence of traditional paper (or now digital) documentation, they constitute, and contribute to, a cognitive map of the terrain that is deeply intuitive, despite its physical lack of substance.

We each have different ways of seeing landscapes and of interpreting what we see and what we feel about them. What richness would we discover, however, if we could interpret the landscape with the full range of our senses? When I walk the crofts with my dog, Deas (Gaelic for elegant and pretty, because she is), I am often struck by how often she pauses, mid-step, to smell the land, the air, the lichen covering the boulders. This less-aware human considers it a memorable occurrence when the natural fragrance of the land intrudes upon my sense of place. Often, it is not so much a smell, as the faintest suggestion of a smell that provokes the memory of a specific situation, a particular place. I remember the sharp clarity of a burst of wild Garlic that fills the air at a certain bend in the path, the giddy aroma of Wild Thyme in bloom on the moor as we stride across it, stirring clouds of blue Heather pollen-dust, or the salty reek of rotting seaweed piled up five hundred metres away on the shore after a winter storm. I don't even want to get distracted to ponder on the many smells of the land that Deas, a Border Collie, apparently finds so fascinating in the hollows and corners of the land, while I walk past, unaware. It seems that only when the scents are extreme do they penetrate our olfactory receptors. How much more of that pervasive aroma-rama would I need to be able to identify in order to navigate my way across the land solely by my sense of smell?

## THE SOVIET MAPS

The map that I hold in my hands just now, however, takes the concept of mapping hidden landscapes to new levels of obsession. Many people will now be aware of the Nazi maps of the UK that were prepared in anticipation of Hitler's invasion, but similar to that non-event, more sinister maps are now known to exist. Like some electrifying twist in a plot by John Le Carré, it is staggering to discover that the Soviet authorities, from the era of Stalin in the 1940s to the time of Gorbachev, managed a colossal operation that secretly mapped the whole world. The most recent maps so far discovered date from 1990. At the scales of from 1 to one million, right down to 1:25,000, many millions of individual maps were produced, using both satellite imagery and clandestine surveys on the ground.[25] Only a casual remark in a conversation with Christopher Fleet, the Curator of maps at the National Library of Scotland, which we later followed up in more detail, led to my awareness of these ephemera. He had mentioned the existence of these maps in earlier works on the mapping of Scotland,[34] and the cartography of the Scottish islands,[35] but the full significance of this had passed me by. The maps of Lewis that I am studying now are intimately familiar in their outlines, but deeper than that basic level, everything is different. To begin with, the legends of all the place names are in Cyrillic script. Important cities and regional centres are labelled in Russian, but all other places are rendered in English phonetic pronunciation, but in Cyrillic lettering so that a Russian speaker could easily read and pronounce them. At first, it is mystifying, then intriguing to recognise ГаЛСОН (Galson), ЌРОСС (Cros), and ХаЙ-БОРе (High Borve), and all the other local places, even the bare-topped headland of Toa Galson (Тоа ГаЛСОН) which would have been a usefully identifiable landmark for an invading army which never arrived.

The detail is incredible, and more scrupulously intense than on most domestic UK maps (there were an estimated 36,000 military mapmakers employed in the production).[35] Close examination shows that in some key locations the width of the road, the load-bearing capacity of a bridge, the depths of rivers and harbours, have been added - specifications that are not annotated on Ordnance Survey maps, but might be useful if you are driving a Soviet tank or piloting a submarine in unfamiliar territory. The map of the west-side of Lewis is fairly innocuous (although Stornoway, a proposed NATO base in the 1970s, is drawn in careful detail). In other parts of the country, and across the globe, military bases and sensitive defensive locations, even secret defence establishments and military harbours, are included, though these are often not depicted on the official maps produced by their own country. The discovery of these secret maps only came about because of the functional collapse of the USSR in 1992. While archives in Russia remained off-limits, there was less scrupulous control in the former so-called satellite states. In Latvia, tonnes of the previously unknown maps, instead of being pulped as ordered, were sold off to an enthusiastic collector who went on to establish a map shop, and through this route, the existence of the maps eventually became public knowledge outwith Russia.[26] When you next mull over the hidden layers of landscape, stop for a second or two to remember that, wherever you are, a Russian agent has moved among your familiar local landscape, adding meticulous detail to the work of their specialist cartographers in the sky, and putting into practice the Cold War Russian proverb, *'trust, but verify'*.

# 10
# The golden pig

To some people,
places speak with a different voice.

I watched him across the gulf of the room from the darkened corner where I stood waiting for the sale to begin. I was sure that he wouldn't notice me staring at him through the constant bustling activity of people and animals, but all the same I guarded my view by turning my head slightly, always ready to smile in another direction if he should look at me directly.

I needn't have bothered of course, for he was quite oblivious to any personal attention. His eyes were firmly centred on the pen of sheep in front of him, measuring, judging, assessing the value of the stock. He spoke to no-one, and on this morning, no-one spoke to him, more from a matter of urgency to settle the work at hand than from any stand-offishness on his part, though God knows he could be morose enough at times. There was just enough strangeness about him for the children to christen him 'Mad MacKay', though none of us had the courage to shout it openly.

When I was a small boy in the same village we would frequently see MacKay wandering alone on the moor. Some said that he was gathering special herbs and plants, for it was known that he knew a lot about natural medicines. Others claimed that he was communing with the animals, and he was certainly more informed than most people about the movements of the birds and the deer, and other mysteries of nature. Still others disparaged him as strange or unhinged, and certainly if you came close enough you could hear him talking aloud, but there was nobody near to reply, for he appeared never to see you. My father's opinion was that he was "a smart man, he just had a bad war." I have to record that 'Mad MacKay' was always gentle with me.

There is always a curious half-light in the livestock mart, a combination of the high roof of darkly-corrugated cladding and the innumerable flickering shadows created by the pillars, posts, and partition walls which divide up the floor space into the web of small pens leading to the auction ring. Perhaps the poor roof windows and the inadequate wall lamps have been left for so long because they contribute to the atmosphere of the establishment, or perhaps the lack of clarity assists the sale of the less impressive beasts; at any rate, none of the décor changes from year to year, to year. It was the time when smoking tobacco in public places was not just permitted, you could be forgiven for thinking that it was a mandatory activity, and the air on a sale day was always heavy with acrid nicotine smoke and the pervasive aroma of rams.

I had decided to pop into the mart on that day to catch some of the main annual ram sale during my lunch break. Though I had no stock to sell that year, and had no intention of buying, it was well known that some of the most interesting animals on view were the owners of the rams, rather than the rams themselves. Take MacKay for instance: it was rumoured that he had once been a nautical pilot for ports on the Amazon River, though to look at him now you wouldn't believe that he had ever been more than ten miles from Brebhig in his entire life. My gaze lifted from the conversation with which I had become involved, and through the slowly milling crowd I could see that MacKay had hardly moved a muscle for the past ten minutes.

He was wrapped in a huge boilersuit of bright orange, which bore the name and logo of an oil exploration company across his shoulders. It was unlikely that he had ever worked for this company in his life, though from some of the stories he told after a couple of drams you could be led to believe that he had been a personal acquaintance of the Chairman of the Board of Directors when they had been working in Africa. Part of the problem was that it is so difficult to separate the fantasy from the reality, for there is no doubt about it that a good many of these old crofters had been familiar at one time with the bars of Panama and the side-streets of Port Said. Though they were making this infrequent visit to town to coincide with the day of the ram sale, it should not be looked upon as any indicator of a completely sedentary existence. Looking around myself at that moment, I was able to identify two old men who had been at the whaling in South Georgia, another grey-haired crofter who had been a lumberjack and later a gold prospector in the upland forests of Canada, and yet another man who had been a contract shearer and sheep farmer in New Zealand before the urge to return to these islands had become too strong for him to resist. There were undoubtedly others among that crowd with strange travelogues to tell.

But MacKay? He was a curious character.

Like many of his generation I knew that he had left the island soon after leaving school to join the merchant navy. Later, in the war against fascism, he had joined the Royal Navy to get some of his own back after two cargo boats had been sunk beneath his feet and he himself was fished out of the Atlantic while so many friends had died. That much was known fact, but in the intervening years, when little or nothing had been heard of him back home, he could have been living anywhere, working at anything. Since he had come home again to stay he lived a fairly solitary life, working away on the croft in all weathers, selling a batch of beautiful lambs every year, and reading any book he could get his hands upon. It was the joke in Brebhig that he kept the mobile library in business, and some said that it was the endless volumes of knowledge which he crammed into his head which made him go crazy a couple of years ago and necessitated his short holiday in a mainland hospital.

I knew that there were plenty of ex-adventurers around that auction ring, and as I looked from face to face, I tried to capture some of the mystery of their hidden lives, but all I could see was rank confusion. One man, having failed to sell his scraggy, short-woolled tup, was now attempting to take it out of the ring by same gateway they had entered, thereby ensuring the maximum congestion and the greatest confusion in the smallest space available. A tall, thin crofter, attempting to enter the ring with his animal, was straining desperately at the length of rope which he had fastened round the beast's neck. His ram, however, had already scented battle and was about to charge at the emerging head of the scraggy ram. As I watched, the scraggy ram recognised the situation and did an astonishingly nimble U-turn back into the ring, pursued by his rival, who seemed at least twice his size. The pantomime developed as the rope snapped tight and the thin crofter slipped on the dirty concrete floor. Before he had time to recover his balance, he was sliding forwards on his back-side as the ram dragged him swiftly in pursuit.

People scattered in surprise as the auctioneer yelled and swore from his wooden box overlooking the ring. It seemed that the thin man would be dragged right into the ring, but his splayed legs stuck like a solid V against the upright posts of the narrow gateway. For a second there was silence as we all watched in anticipation as his knuckles tightened and whitened around the length of rope, but the abrupt, violent jerk brought the ram to a standstill long enough to allow two men standing near to each grab a horn. The spell was broken, and this resolution was greeted with a burst of noise and laughter, though the auctioneer was still swearing roundly at their incompetence.

In the short burst of hilarity before the ram sale re-commenced, I looked round and met the laughing eyes of my friends across the width of the room: but I noticed MacKay had still not moved one inch. He stood at the edge of the auction ring, one foot slightly raised on the first bar of the railings, his hands clasped, and his elbows leaning heavily on the topmost rail. With a look that was neither amused nor dismissive, he seemed to be measuring the worth of the ram by its ability to drag the thin man through the bars of the railings. There was neither humour nor contempt in his final assessment, and as the next ram was led into the sale he turned and elbowed his way away from the ringside towards the back of the room. I watched his back move through the crowd and guessed that he was making for the covered pens in the adjoining room, probably to bring in one of his own rams into the sale. But as I watched, a voice spoke into my ear, and when I turned to greet the speaker I lost sight of MacKay.

For a minute or two I caught up with the news from my old school friend, Iain, always humorous and frequently with scathing observations to make on life and death, and everything in between. We were just beginning to settle into a discussion of the merits and demerits of Texel tups when even the raucous din of the auction mart was muted by the distinctive, if somewhat incongruous, sound of a hunting horn. Even Murdigen, the auctioneer, was moved to open-mouthed, silent, astonishment, and it seemed for a few seconds that each eye in the building swivelled in its socket towards the rear of the shedding pens, where MacKay stood resplendent in his glory.

As if to confirm to the sceptics that they had actually heard a hunting horn, he blew the curled brass instrument again, bringing a dangerously red flush to his already florid face with the intensity of his musical effort. But the hunting horn could well be considered to be the least of MacKay's extravagances on that day, for the sight which greeted us now was himself in a light blue military-style uniform, complete with gold braiding, yellow scrubbing-brush epaulettes, and an officer's white-topped cap with a heavy, brassy insignia above his forehead.

At the second sounding of the horn, the business of the auction ring had come to a hesitant standstill and as MacKay walked towards the ring the perplexed onlookers melted before him to form a path as surely defined as the splitting of the Red Sea. Only when this unusual spectacle had begun to register with the crowd did I notice that MacKay was leading a large ram by his side, and surely the spectacle of the ram was even more astonishing than that of MacKay himself. The ram was a huge, hornless Texel with the very short, tight, curly wool typical of his breed, and it had obviously been dipped in one of the fancy new dipping fluids which contain a chemical dye, for the entire woollen surface of the ram was a vibrant yellow in colour. The normally black hooves of the animal had been painted with a canary-yellow varnish, and the chalk-white cord in MacKay's hand ran to a thick collar formed by a broad yellow ribbon, tied in an elaborate bow at the back of the animal's neck. The normally short wool had been newly shorn, and the pink skin shone through the yellow haze to produce a curious rippling quality as the animal walked, displaying its solid muscular shoulders as proudly as any champion boxer. The overall impression was of a giant golden pig being taken for a walk by the Admiral of the Fleet.

MacKay and his animal strode into the ring and before an incredulous audience he sounded the hunting horn for the third time.

"Sebastian Cortez the First, pedigree Texel tup," he announced at the top of his voice, and this human interjection had the effect of breaking the dream-time spell which had held the rapt attention of the whole gathering.

First a brave chuckle could be heard from deep within the circle of the crowd, which was met by full-throated laughter from the opposite side of the ring, and within seconds there was a growing chorus of hilarity which must have set a curious precedent for that normally functional and utilitarian building. It seemed that only a confused local drunk, and Murdigen himself, the auctioneer and owner of the mart, were not infected by the fun and the absurdity of the spectacle, apart, of course, for MacKay himself, who stood straight-backed and straight-faced in the centre of the ring with his prize animal.

The laughter, however, died down as quickly as it had sprung up when Murdigen began to shout and abuse almost everyone in a torrent of creative invective which seemed only to fuel his anger rather than release it. He swore at MacKay for being there, and for bringing mockery to his establishment, he swore at his ring-side hands for their inability to remove MacKay from the ring faster than he had entered it, and he swore at the general mass of his prospective customers for what he saw as their encouragement and collaboration with MacKay in this horrendous attack on his professional integrity. Prompted by their boss, the ring-side hands tried to hustle MacKay out of the exit gate, and the huge golden pig, sensing, some might have thought, a latent hostility towards its owner, dropped its mantle of docility and began to chase both of the workmen alternately round the ring, while MacKay folded his arms across his chest and calmly surveyed the proceedings. Rams, in general, are never to be fully trusted, and the auction attendants were not about to put that to the test. The general hilarity increased towards a crescendo and was added to by cat-calls and the very vocal encouragement of the crowd.

Finally, when he could take it no longer, Murdigen leapt out of the auctioneer's booth, his fleshy face pillar-box red, and his mouth white-rimmed with a fulminating spittle. Snatching a long-handled crook from a ring-side observer, he began to beat the golden pig about the back and shoulders, finally succeeding in driving it towards and through the exit gate. As the tail of the animal disappeared, MacKay came out of his torpidity to rescue his four-legged friend, and Murdigen turned his stick-waving wrath on old MacKay himself. I was close to the entry gate at this time, and as the flailing stick caught the old man on the side of the head and knocked him to the sawdust floor, I leapt over the railings to restrain the auctioneer. Things had gone far enough.

Fortunately, there were several others of the same opinion as myself, and as I stepped between the two men, others appeared, to lay hold of Murdigen and to help old MacKay to his feet. But Murdigen wasn't to be placated so easily. He struggled and wrestled with his captors, shouting and swearing at MacKay, who stood quietly alone, mopping the blood on his head with a white handkerchief and an impressive serenity.

"Get him out of here! He's as mad as a hatter! I don't want to see him in here again! Donald, get him out of here! Show him the road!"

Donald, his employee, was already sufficiently embarrassed by the whole episode to have second thoughts about tackling MacKay again, but as Murdigen continued to yell, he moved forwards a pace or two.

MacKay raised his hand with his palm facing outwards, and stopped Donald abruptly in his tracks, for even in the comic military uniform of an Amazonian Pilot, MacKay could still command respect. As I stood between them, MacKay reached into an inside pocket and solemnly produced a piece of folded paper.

"You say I'm mad," he said quietly to Murdigen, "but I have a paper here which says otherwise."

He continued to look directly, eyeball-to-eyeball with Murdigen, but he handed me the piece of paper to read. It was his certificate of discharge from the mental hospital, and it was signed and dated by the specialist fourteen months previously.

"*I* have that paper which testifies that I am of sane mind. Do *you* have as much? He said to Murdigen, "Or *you*?"

I was at a loss to answer that question, but in the end, it was not needed, for MacKay picked up his hat from the sawdust-covered floor and walked with effortless dignity, slowly and deliberately, out of the ring in the direction of his now disappeared ram. The wreckage of the sale was left behind him like the human jetsam of a high tide.

# 11
# Interlinking layers

## THE EYE THAT SEES

Once, many years ago, when I arrived in South Island, New Zealand, to begin a lecture tour of campuses, I was told to expect a traditional Māori welcome after my drive from the airport. The format went like this. An elder of the local *Iwi* (people) would issue a welcoming challenge, telling me that I was now in *their* land. I would respond by telling them where I came from. A traditional Māori song would be sung to me, again I would sing my own song in reply (I had several

Kiwi volunteers on hand who could sing for me by proxy!).
I would then offer the elders a small gift, and if my gift was
accepted, we could formally begin my visit. I asked what would
happen if my gift was refused, and I was told, "Then we have
a problem!" The Māori have a strong spiritual bond with the
land - *Papatūānuku* (the Earth mother) and the land, soil, and
water are regarded as *taonga* (treasures) for all the people to
enjoy. As a guardian of these treasures, it was explained to me
that the elder would introduce himself by giving the name of
the mountain and the river with which he personally identified,
before saying his own name. My greeting in response was in
Gaelic, (which made the anticipated impact) and fortunately
my offering was accepted, so we celebrated by sharing some
food and drink. Afterwards, I remarked how moving and
appropriate the ceremony had been. Something about the
glint in the eyes of that elder alerted me, and when I pushed
him, he admitted that he knew I would appreciate it because
he had done his homework on me. He had checked my profile
on the internet! It is something almost like alchemy to divine
that connection of Earth-allegiance over twelve thousand miles
of fibre and routers, but to empathise in person was so much
more satisfying.

As an islander and an academic, a person who is closely
involved in both the natural environment and the human
culture of this place, I have occasionally asked my colleagues
if they recognise a specific epistemology of place. There is
certainly a specific theory of knowledge that we use to describe
and analyse the inter-linked land-based systems of the natural
environment.[94] Is there a multidisciplinary but interconnected

way of thinking about islands (to give one of my particular interests) that is systematically alternative to the way in which we learn about non-island places? And if that is so, what is it that differentiates the ways of learning? Predictably, the responses vary, and it seems likely to me that often they are conditioned, as Neil Gunn speculated in his essay, *Landscape Inside*,[73] that in the shadowy ground between individual experience and general experience, where '... *in this particular region of the mind, place and people meet. The outer and the inner landscapes merge.*'

Intriguingly, I have also read that, '*In the Apache language, the root word for land is the same as the word for mind.*'[105] Elsewhere Gunn has written that, taken together, these realisations produce, '... *a moment of heightened understanding by going beyond the boundaries of conscious and limited intellect...*'.[44] To my colleagues, I have likened this to re-reading a favourite book several years later and discovering new meanings because the intervening years between the first and the second reading have contextualised the knowledge accumulated in the interim. This might be similar to the phenomenon by which, having been made aware of something for the first time, we suddenly begin to see examples almost everywhere we look, and we wonder why we haven't seen it before. Is it really a new phenomenon or is it just something that we lacked the specific awareness to notice previously?

The landscape is simply our image of the land, but the land changes, and so does the landscape. Things in nature are not always what they seem to be at first sight. Harmless hoverflies might avoid predation by imitating bees and wasps with their cryptic black-and-yellow colouring, and their sophisticated imitation is betrayed only by the very careful identification of a faint vein running parallel to the trailing edge of the wings. In this way they pretend to potential predators that they are a species that is more to be reckoned with than a simple fly. In dense vegetation or solar darkness, a thermal imaging camera can use infrared energy, light that is not available to us in our normally visible human spectrum, to make evident the details of species that pass within metres of us without our knowledge. At a still deeper level, the distinctiveness of individual chemical and mineralogical signatures of even 'common' rocks like granite define their provenance like lithic fingerprints and can tell us obscure details such as the age, original temperature, and depth of formation from the parent magma.

In some circumstances we can even use these chemical signatures to compare with those obtained from the analysis of archaeological remains, to determine if the living individual is likely to have lived in that area or was an 'outsider' from a terrain with different geochemical ratios. Encoded within that solid rock may also be an invisible magnetic attribution which the cooling magma acquired from the contemporary polarity of the planet Earth, which is distinctive of the geographical position of the rock as it crystallised into granite. Even in this, however, appearances are deceptive, because the variations between True North and Magnetic North mean that over tens of millions of years (comparatively rapidly in geological time) almost nowhere is the landscape in exactly the same position in relation to the initial terrain. The fixed geographical point on the surface of the globe that indicates True North is usually quite a different location from the wandering Magnetic North that drifts around the northern extremities of Earth, driven by magmatic convection currents deep within the planet. Still more incredibly, at frequent geological intervals the Earth flips the polarity of these magnetic currents, with 'north' becoming 'south' and vice versa. Plotting these movements of the shifting magnetic field is one of the sources of evidence that led to discovery of 'drifting' continents and the dynamic interactions of plate tectonics that explain the stretching of crustal regions to form new oceans and their compression elsewhere to create continental-scale mountain ranges.

Nor is the mystery of disappearing continents confined to the realms of the sub-microscopic examination of atomic particles and their physical patterns of invisible radiation, magnetism, and chemical re-combinations. Sometimes the evidence of our own eyes is deceiving. A good friend in Bhutan told me a funny story at his own expense about one of these disappearing lands. When he arrived alone at Heathrow Airport as an early teenage maths prodigy to study in London about forty years ago, no one was there to meet him. He sat on a bench amid the endlessly moving crowds, waiting to be greeted by his university host, but nobody came. After a while he became fascinated by the continual stream of people who entered the narrow boxroom beside him. Thousands went through the gateway to this fantastical world, but nobody ever re-emerged. It was the first time that he had seen a lift. Throughout the Highlands and Islands of Scotland there are probably several hundred inconspicuous *sìthean*, little conical green hillocks of piled-up stones that are known in English as 'fairy knolls'. There are two *sìthean* in my village alone, and these are recognised in northern folklore as the abode of the little people – our Nordic cousins might call them Trolls – into which the fiddlers of legend descended into the depths of the land to party for a whole Earth-year as if it were merely a day that they spent. In a way, these *sìthean* are lithic elevators to the underworld, and few who ever venture there are fortunate enough to return safely.[65]

As young adults, working on a calm summer day in a roadless glen of the West Highland mainland, a friend and I became convinced that we could hear people shouting to us from among the ruins of a village from which the inhabitants had been removed during the notorious Highland Clearances. It was a warm, sunny day and rational consideration made us laugh at that experience, but the laughter was muted, and the event left us unsettled. To recreate a landscape image from memory is to imagine it, and in that imagination we both invent new versions and also suddenly recognise old subtleties with a growing importance not immediately apparent in the original viewing. In his classic book, *A Vertebrate Fauna of the Outer Hebrides*, John Alexander Harvie-Brown wrote,

> '... *often thus do the wondrous effects of light and shade, and the weird twilights of the long, long summer nights, recur to us in memory almost as vividly as they did in nature*...'. [47]

That astonishing clarity of proximity in the landscape
of the Scottish islands can give everything that you see a
sparkling freshness: from the sticky droplets on the leaves of
a fly-trapping Common Butterwort, to the myriad flashes
of the dew that will soak your trouser legs as effectively as a
downpour, to the intriguing glittering reflections of the sun
on mica crystals in a rockface a couple of kilometres away.
Sometimes the extreme clarity of the air seems to shrink
the landscape, so that even landforms that you know to be
a certain distance away appear to be much closer than they
actually are, as you will soon find out when you decide to walk
to them across the moor.

In her book, *Pilgrim at Tinker Creek*,[28] Annie Dillard described
many aspects of becoming intimately acquainted with a
small area of land, including gaining an awareness of that
'other landscape' through 'seeing' a foreground of flies and
birds against a backdrop of an out-of-focus world. Those
complex layers of perspective are often apparent in the open
landscapes of the Hebrides, where it is quite common to see
the weather – the vertical rain and the horizontal wind, the
spreading skyscape of soft sunlight – hours or minutes before
the physical sensation arrives to envelop you. Living among the
layers of this land can educate you in a fine awareness of the
distinction between being 'vague' and being 'elusive'.

In 1773 James Hutton, often regarded as the founder of
modern geology, wrote to his friend Dr James Lind (the first
cousin of another Dr James Lind who pioneered the cure for
scurvy at sea), about those fragmentary remnants of Earth
history as the latter prepared to accompany Captain James

Cook on an exploratory voyage to the Antipodes. In his letter, Hutton urged his friend to bring him evidence that would enable him to interpret and understand the history of those faraway lands.

> '... *the shortest and best way of doing this is to take samples... however small the samples are... a bag of gravel is a history to me, and with the above will tell wondrous tales, in this manner I may yet be mineralogist to the expedition, almost to as good a purpose as if I had made the voyage... I need say no more of this; only, mind, a bag of gravel is worth a bag of gold...'* [13]

One of the (many) benefits of an education in geological science is the ability to be able to perceive different ways of seeing the world. A common adage is that "the present is the key to the past" and from this geomorphological base, my world evolved. From a very early age I was subsumed into increasingly diverse ways of being immersed in the landscape: the shapes of hills, their names and meanings, and the fabric of their construction. When I was ten years old, I returned from a month-long school camp in the Trossachs with an unliftable suitcase full of rock samples and a newly-discovered passion for geology in all its forms. By eighteen I was in Aberdeen embarking on a degree in geology, and my Advisor of Studies, Dr Bill Fraser, said at our first meeting, "so, you want to be a geologist?" I nodded my head, trying not to be too enthusiastic. He smiled and said, "There is one born every minute." He was a very fine geologist himself, so I knew the comment was a non sequitur, and in a very Scottish way, it reassured me. The following year his induction began, "So, you're still here…?" and I knew that I was exactly where I should be. Just a few years later I was studying not just the rocks, but the chemistry of the minerals in those rocks. As my interest had deepened, so also had it broadened to include the botany associated with different rock types, the fauna dependent on those vegetational habitats, as well as the human culture and derivation of the place names of the areas of land that I walked across. In a very practical way, I was learning that the natural environment, and our interactions with it, are constructed of minutely interdependent overlapping networks of complex adaptive systems. These intimate relationships may have obvious consequences, or their complexity might be so intertwined that our understanding is currently only partially realised. Complex adaptive systems have a number of distinctive features that govern and explain the often-bewildering cause-and-effect reactions that produce the constant changes and readjustments that we observe in nature. This is not the place to elaborate the intricate mechanisms that influence complex adaptive systems, but three quick points are perhaps relevant, if not essential to raise: feedback, emergent properties, and stability domains.[71]

In the simplest of explanations, changes in these systems are directed by feedback mechanisms. Positive feedback accentuates change, encouraging a growing emphasis in one direction, for good or for ill, whereas negative feedback counteracts the impact of change and attempts to restore system stability. For our current purposes, the effects of feedback can contribute strongly to how we talk about and think about our relationships with the land. It seems that 'the general public' have multiple ways of thinking about moorland,[64] with perhaps marginally more people regarding the tranquillity of moorland landscape as positive and benign, rather than bleak and desolate, but there is little evidence that any of the respondents have any direct or analytical experience of the land that they have categorised. The more that people talk simplistically about 'barren' moor and 'wild land' when they in fact mean terrain that is poor for agriculture even though it is ecologically rich, the more the stereotype is reinforced. Eventually, by constant repetition, any contrasting argument is marginalised, and the language of society becomes conditioned to believing that land is worthless. Only through championing the counter-narrative will the negative feedback eventually restore our values of the land to a more balanced perspective. Part of this counter-narrative is to remind people that places like the Highlands and Islands of Scotland can only possibly be considered 'wild' because the people who used to live there and managed a wider biodiversity than exists there just now, were forcibly removed to satisfy misguided ideas of economic 'improvement'. Only when the counter-narrative of our conversation is valued for itself will the complementary negative feedback of practical action begin to make a significant impact upon how we sensitively manage the *whole* landscape.

This is not a trivial point, for although a great deal of our understanding of the landscape is compartmentalised, both physically and mentally, it is only in the fullness of the total ecosystem that the system functions effectively. My wife's uncle Roddy could name all the stances along our shoreline that were favourable for rock-fishing in the Atlantic, for in his youth he had been a keen fisherman, but he was a little more vague about naming the moorland topography. My old neighbour, Murdo, however, had been to the moor countless times gathering livestock and could give the place names that differentiated localities that were closely adjacent but completely different in their aspects. Artificial designations that humans concoct to facilitate easier administration, such as nature reserves, Environmentally Sensitive Areas, Special Areas of Conservation, and many other such designations, may seem convenient, but the species needing protection are not aware of those lines on a map. Disturbingly few individuals of the population of a threatened species select the habitat of a protected area, and so the requirement for sensitive land management across the wider countryside is necessary for their survival. The scattered localities of protected areas are analogous to drifting lifeboats from a sunken ship, separated by hostile sea and the wreckage of the parent ship.

In many traditional landscapes, different areas of land are used at different times of the year, and the shifting management practices are crucial to complement each other in order to maintain the healthy balance of the whole. To gain an appreciation of this, look at the extensive hinterland that is the catchment of even a relatively-modest river system. The small village river in front of my house is scarcely two metres wide in most parts, yet its dendritic network extends like a hydric representation of an ancient tree, spreading far out into the peatland catchment. It is barely eight kilometres from source to ocean in a straight line, but the sinuous stream winds and twists in complex loops as if reluctant to leave the softness of the peat in exchange for the rocky shore. The total length of the main burn is probably nearer thirteen kilometres, draining in excess of twenty-two square kilometres of terrain, and the aggregated total distance of the countless small tributaries and vein-like feeder rivulets is several hundred kilometres in length. This catchment of a small stream unites the high moorland and the dynamically-changing shore, the deep peat bog and the sandy grassland, the agricultural croft land, and the areas of domestic settlement in a natural footprint of reciprocity that needs no mere line on a map to explain itself. Each part has its own function and identity but is connected to every other part by innumerable small associations that we are still discovering. The secrets of this landscape are hidden in plain sight, and I am again reminded of stories about indigenous communities withholding medical cures and botanical remedies from the 'settlers' who appropriated their land so that though the thieves might acquire the big machine, they did not get the operating instructions.[52]

Emergent properties are more difficult to explain, but, basically, they are fundamental effects of the synergy of the system as a whole, that are not found in any of the component parts alone. Conceptually this might be expressed by some cliché such as 'producing something that is greater than the sum of the parts'. In practice, this is often much more difficult to identify than the simple theory would suggest. As an example of this, we might return to the concept of *buntanas*. This deep-seated sense of belongingness is much more than just a fond identification with the place where you were born or grew up, more than the comforting knowledge of the closeness of the extended family and neighbours. It encompasses the idea of a shared culture and history, even though there will continue to be contested interpretations of that history, and a shared dependency on the natural environment, whether or not we value or squander, recognise or refute the resources provided by that environment. Each of these factors has an importance in shaping our identity, but only when we start to join these components together do we begin to see the emergence of that extraordinary awareness of *buntanas* and gain the first glimpse of the depth of our connections with the land that has formed us.

Which leads us, perhaps inevitably, to the identification of stability domains, which are described as system states that are characterised by natural or social processes that tend to keep the system in those states. In terms of our relationships to the land, stability domains might be those 'special places' that we return to again and again, even if only in our memories. They might also be those particular layers of belonging within the landscape that form a sort of terrestrial 'comfort blanket', a place of reassurance or solace, or simply a horizon that we recognise as a place that is welcoming, where we can relax. As Neil Gunn would have put it, a place where our inner and outer landscapes can comfortably meet and merge.[43]

Or, as the American writer Wendell Berry wrote,

> 'No expert knows everything about every place,
> not even everything about any place'.[6]

… but getting down among the many layers of the land and picking up the pieces is probably a good way to make a start.

# 12
# Picking up the pieces

## Even for the initiated, there are layers of understanding in each place.

I suppose that I am one of the lucky ones. We have deep roots in this place. My family has lived on our croft for at least seven generations. It's not a big piece of land, and though the soil is shallow, what it lacks in nutrients it compensates for in the volume of groundwater. Making any sort of income from this land is hard enough and making a decent living from the land alone is impossible, but life is more than income, and the

views of the landscape in every direction are priceless to me.
The croft is on land that is owned by the whole community,
so we pay the rent to our own company and get a fair hearing
when there are discussions about potential development
opportunities to be considered. Having said that, you can't live
on just beautiful scenery; jobs are not always easy to find, so I
was glad when Willie, one of our crofting neighbours, offered
to help me out. Willie has a few sheep, but his main income is
working as the Head Gillie on a neighbouring sporting estate,
and there is very little about catching a salmon or shooting a
Red Deer on which you would be able to instruct him. He had
heard that the estate was looking for a casual worker for the
summer to help out with a steady stream of paying guests who
wanted to escape to the country temporarily and get back to
nature by walking on the moor and killing wildlife. I was a
student, and he knew that I was looking for a job, so he put in
a good word for me. To be truthful, he was also doing himself
a favour because he dreaded the appointment of some random
urban student whom he would have to babysit all summer. At
least I came with a set of well-known risks and advantages, so
with any luck it might be a reasonably pleasant few months for
both of us.

*     *     *     *     *

As I watched, Willie smiled quietly as he tugged in agitation
at the hem of his jacket. It was a soft green-and-brown
Harris Tweed sports jacket, worn at the edges, and curiously
shapeless, though it seemed to fit him with casual elegance.

166

"There he is, there." he said softly to DonDon, the second-gillie. "He's at it now!"

We all leaned towards the small, dirt-stained window of the basement gear-shed for a better view. Willie was gazing with a satisfied, almost triumphal expression. DonDon exhibited unashamed, open-mouthed, amazement. Together we all peered through the four tiny panes of the square window that was inconspicuously set near the ground level, looking out over a flower bed that edged the base of the castle walls. ("It is not a castle really," Willie would frequently say, "simply a big house that got out of control and developed grandiose notions.")

Through the glass we could see a man on all fours, crawling about on the big front lawn. He appeared to be searching diligently for something that was lost in the short grass. As we watched, a young lady strode over to the crawling man. They seemed to exchange a few heated words. She pulled at his jacket, trying to get him to stand on his feet, but he brushed her hand away abruptly. Again, they exchanged words, then the woman turned about and marched off sharply in the direction from which she had appeared. As she disappeared from view, Willie and DonDon could no longer suppress their laughter, and it came tumbling out, bubbling out, into the confined space of the gear shed. Between tears and gasps, DonDon managed to say. "How did you manage it, Willie?"

"Ach, it was quite easy really," the Head Gillie replied, "I've seen his type before many a time. You just need to know how to set the bait."

\*　　\*　　\*　　\*　　\*

167

In front of me, Willie threw the tackle bag and laid the rods
onto the spiky grass. The paying guest dropped down beside
the gear, struggling a little for breath though he was barely
half the age of the gillie. (I have always thought that it is rather
incongruous to call a man older than your father a gillie - 'boy'
- and when I was travelling in the southern USA and first heard
black-skinned servants being called 'boy' the comparison was
not lost on me.) Even before he had managed to fully regain his
breath, however, the guest had launched into another story of
his bravado.

"... It was a bit like a modern-day pirate raid," he explained
to us (Willie briefly departed from his task of setting up the
fishing rods to roll his eyes to me, indicating that the client was
possibly the least pirate-like of any of the paying guests to visit
the estate that he could remember.)

"... from the time we started until we cashed in the bonds, it
was probably only forty-five minutes, perhaps thirty-five ...."

Willie continued to assemble the gear in his slow, methodical
way, listening with one ear to the monologue with a practised
detachment. This was our third day of escorting this particular
guest. Willie said that he didn't really mind that the man was
hopeless at the fishing ... (or should he have called him 'the
boy', for to Willie, although the client was a grown man in
stature, there was a good deal of the irresponsibility of an
adolescent about his behaviour?) No, he didn't mind, in fact,
if they did no fishing at all, though it was a pity to waste a
good day like this, a calm surface on the loch, mild air, with
a gentle, soft sunlight. After all, the guest had paid for his
sporting holiday. He could do as much, or as little, as he liked

with his own money. The big question was, why did he have
to talk all the time? Talk, talk, talk. The man had an opinion
on everything, and he seemed obligated to share it. Still, Willie
was accustomed by long experience to filter out the ramblings
of rich visitors - he had developed a skill at following the
gist of the story by picking up one word in every five, or by
latching on to the key phrases and turning the tables by asking
a judicious question at the appropriate time. He really didn't
mind if they talked a lot, so long as they didn't expect him to
join in with it and contribute the same level of inanity. Willie
was a quiet man. I was new to the routine, simply doing a
student job to earn money during the holidays to help meet the
bills accrued during the rest of the year and save something for
future plans, so I simply watched and listened in fascination.

There were two main problems with this type of guest. Firstly,
Willie didn't like them to be too talkative when they were going
after the stags. Any unnecessary noise at the wrong time and
they might as well not set out onto the hill at all. Secondly,
if they were really feckless at the stalking or the fishing, they
wouldn't get anything to show to their friends, and this would
eventually rebound on himself. When he anticipated that this
was going to happen, he felt compelled to engineer a catch
in order to salvage some pride for the guest and to perhaps
encourage them to come back for another season (or at least
recommend it to their friends, for there were occasionally some
fine conversations to be had among those visitors.)

"And what was the purpose of this ...... raid?" interposed
Willie, breaking into the flow of the pirate story at just the
right moment, as he finished assembling the second rod and

tried a dry cast over the edge of the long pool. I tried to look busy, but I edged closer to hear more clearly.

"The purpose?" asked the guest incredulously. "The purpose was to secure total rights to all the available stock and to sell it off before the real value was discovered, thereby securing four-and-a-half million pounds in our own bank account. Think of it! Four-and-a-half million! Not bad for barely half an hour's work." (Willie noted that the time taken for the pirate raid was decreasing with the repetition of the story.)

"So, you buy up stocks of...?"

"Guavas" interjected the guest.

"Aye, you buy next year's guavas from farmers, who don't yet have them to sell to you anyway. Then you wait until the people who need to buy guavas for the supermarkets start to panic that there won't be any guavas available next year. Then you sell them all off for a higher price?"

"That's right." said the guest, waggling his rod, attempting a dry-fly cast that horrified me with its gaucheness. ("It was a bit like beating an invisible carpet with a wooden stick that is too big for you to hold." Willie later said to DonDon.)

"But all the time you never really had any guavas anyway," continued Willie, "and you don't even know if the farmers will ever have any to give you when the harvest time comes?" (He marvelled at the way some folk found to make a living - a bit like those people who had once tried to sell him a watch on a platform in the London Underground. "Why would anyone want to buy a watch in a railway station?" he asked me.)

"It's called 'the Futures Market' - it's a whole industry.

It's complex.'" said the guest, who then fortunately lapsed
into a relative silence as he battled with the flexibilities of a
carbon-fibre fishing rod that seemed to have a private life of its
own.

"A bit like him paying good money in advance for a salmon that
he will never get, no matter how long he waits," Willie gently
whispered to me under his breath.

*     *     *     *     *

By the fifth day (still without the hint of a fish) things
had pretty much come to a head. Despite the fact that his
holiday-companions had met with a large measure of success
(both the men and the women) Willie's client had yet to
notch up so much as a serious nibble on his line. While the
rest of the party were starting to relax into a self-satisfied
holiday indolence and were lazily attempting to improve their
fishing technique (with varying degrees of finesse, it has to be
admitted) the 'futures dealer' was steadily working himself into
an unhealthy lather. His highly-competitive streak could not
come to terms with his singular lack of sporting success, and it
seemed that his only outlet for this embarrassment was to score
points over other people. There was nothing specifically said,
but he gave off a definite 'atmosphere' that rubbed people up
the wrong way. He was particularly piqued that the wife of his
business partner had managed to land four decent-sized fish,
despite not knowing one end of the rod from the other. All
of the other gillies gave the man a pleasant smile and a subtle

body-swerve at the morning preparations in the tackle room, leaving him solely to the care of Willie, who was well known for his even-tempered patience. I was learning the ropes from Willie, so I saw the whole story develop in slow motion. Even his business companions seemed to be less comfortable in his presence (it is a little difficult to swap experiences on the finer points of technique with one whose understanding of technique is so obviously lacking.) Worst of all, it seemed that a rift had emerged between himself and his young lady (Willie didn't enquire too closely about the nature of their relationship). She too had managed to catch a fine salmon. There was no doubt that she had also become aware of the hidden smiles and the sly digs at her partner's expense, and she had been hurt that his response to her helpful suggestions had been for him to become even more difficult to mix with.

Up at the loch that day, there was a tolerable silence between the three of us. Willie leaned quietly against a large outcrop of rock, teasing tobacco flakes from a battered tin and rolling with precision a strong, thin cigarette. We were enjoying the dappled light of the coming evening where the calm of the loch met the ripples of the river mouth. Twenty metres away the guest was flailing the water lackadaisically with his fishing line. When Willie began to detect that the client was getting restless, and when it began to look as though we might soon be heading back for the castle with an empty net yet again, I got the sense that Willie thought that it might be time for him to intervene. With a slow, unhurried movement, I saw him dip a hand into his jacket pocket. Drawing it out again carefully, he scattered some small pellets across the placid surface of the pool. The guest hardly noticed the event until a curious thing occurred which astonished me, and even the guest could hardly fail to ignore it.

Within a few seconds of Willie scattering the pellets, an inordinate number of fish began to appear at the surface of the pool. They came up splashing and bubbling, some even leaping clean out of the water with an audible 'plop' of excitement. With the same unhurried aloofness, Willie sowed another handful of pellets. This time the reaction was even more pronounced, boiling and tumbling with an audible effervescence. For several seconds, fish seemed to leap in every direction, then the pool slowly went calm again. The guest stood bolt upright on the riverbank, aware that something was happening, but unable to explain what it was. At that point there was a frenetic tugging on the line of Willie's fixed rod, propped up along the bank on a shooting stick and weighed down by a large boulder. With the skilful calm of a man who had been waiting expectantly for the call, Willie lifted the fixed rod and reeled in a frolicking salmon.

I was delighted with the turn of events, but the guest was almost beside himself with excitement. (So much so that Willie admitted later that he feared that he had over-done his casualness.)

"That must be nearly twenty pounds!" the man gasped at last, "What did you do there? What did you scatter on the pool?"

Without speaking, Willie again reached into his jacket pocket and displayed a hand full of small, hard, blackish pellets. The guest looked quizzical.

"Rabbit droppings!" said Willie, "The salmon just love it! It has to be used on them about this time of the early evening, and you have to gather it up very early in the morning, while the dew is still wet on it, but when you get the right conditions, it works wonderfully. I collected these on the front lawn of the castle garden this morning, just in case, you might say."

Slowly we wound up our gear and I began to pack it away for the long walk back to the Landrover. Willie was probably already thinking about what might be waiting for his dinner, and the guest was thinking about how best he might re-tell this story to his own advantage, but I had a definite feeling that this story was not yet finished.

*    *    *    *    *

"So, is that what he's collecting?" said DonDon, "Just the rabbit droppings?"

"So it seems," replied Willie, "though I will be collecting something a bit more substantial from Kenny. I had a bet on with him that I would have yon man on his knees on the front lawn before the end of the week! Twenty pounds it was. Ahh, here they come now."

As we watched through the small window of the gear shed, we saw the morning gathering of fishing guests and their partners come round the corner on their way to the waiting Land Rovers. We saw them stop abruptly, to goggle unbelievably at the man crawling over the grass looking for small, black, rabbit droppings to fill the plastic bag that he carried in his left hand.

174

He was picking up the pieces with studious concentration.
I saw Willie nudge DonDon and give a particular chuckle to
see the look on the face of Kenny, the third-gillie, as he slowly
realised the significance of what we were all looking at. Twenty
pounds down the drain! As the group moved away, towards the
waiting vehicles, Willie and DonDon left our sheltering place in
the gear shed to join the daily party.

"Well, you learn something every day," DonDon said to me
reflectively, "I never knew that salmon would bite at that
stuff."

"Neither did I." chortled Willie.

We both spun around to look at Willie more intently.

He shrugged.

"I filled my pocket with some of those feed-pellets that my
brother-in-law uses in the sea-cages on the salmon farm over
at Trollbhig. The fish go fair daft for them over there, and
I knew that if we got them jumping, there would be a good
chance that we could hook into something in their excitement.
Anyway, that young lad needed taking down a peg or two,
and I figured that I might as well make a couple of quid out
of it - as a commercial side-line you might say." He turned to
DonDon with a gentle smile. "Keep quiet about it and I'll see
that you get a nice dram tonight." And with that he turned
aside and walked across the lawn to coax his paying guest off
his knees and get ready for the day ahead.

✳     ✳     ✳     ✳     ✳

I learned a lot that summer, firstly from Willie about appreciating the moor, and wildlife, and the sheer wonder that comes from the pervasive yet forever incomplete awareness of being immersed in the environment of a place that you really love. Then I also learned a lot about myself. Some of this I suppose I already knew, other things began to make sense once I had started to piece together the various bits of my life, and still other revelations about myself caught me by surprise. I discovered, for instance, that I didn't need to seek the bright city lights to follow my dreams, and in fact this was counterproductive. The components of my dreams were all around me. I adjusted the curriculum of my university course slightly to include a couple of 'elective' modules that would be considered eccentric in the discipline for anyone seeking the best 'professional' CV but made perfect sense to me in terms of my growing self-awareness. I suggested to my girlfriend that we move back to the island, and to my delight, she agreed. I have found rewards that were never even hinted at in my previous dreams. Now I have started my own small business offering environmental 'photo-safaris', and when my paying clients occasionally ask me what 'brought me home' to live in this unique landscape, I enigmatically respond, "Oh, you know, just picking up the pieces".

# Epilogue

Quite frequently, when my affiliation with the land becomes known, someone in the group will ask me their 'challenging question'. Often it is about whether 'you have to be born there' to understand the ways of the land, or can a measure of profound understanding be acquired by someone from 'elsewhere'? The answer to the latter part is, of course, that a deep appreciation can be learned by everybody, it just takes some people a little longer to identify with the land. Even people born into families of several generations of crofters or farmers need to learn the intimacies of that local relationship, and not everyone manages it with equal success. I believe, however, that the potential is inherent in all of us. Every individual human is at times withdrawn from, and at other moments deeply and irrevocably connected to a certain place. Whether we always recognise this association is another issue. I have discovered (probably due to habituation) that even in the last few seconds before the total darkness of a Hebridean winter evening, I am perfectly sure-footed walking the subtle and sinuous paths on our own croft (although I prefer a scintillating walk at dawn with summer approaching). My dog walks with me, and I remember the approximate moment that I discovered that not everyone gives commands to their sheepdog in Gaelic (so, I wondered, how do they properly understand what you mean?). That is an acquired relationship (both with the land and the dog) that not everyone attains.

Surprisingly, other common questions are about 'what makes a place special' and 'how will I recognise that a place is special'? My only possible response is that the questioners will know it when they find it, or else they have not yet found it. There is a moment of connection at the sublime meeting of the inner and the outer landscapes that generates an intimate understanding of pure delight, or utter fear, or simply of the inherent serenity of the place. There is no 'correct' way to precisely define the nature of the land that you view, because the total experience is different for everybody, and therefore any definition will, by its very utterance, be imprecise, fleeting, and intensely personal. Although I don't subscribe to the idea personally, I can understand a little about how some of my friends can describe their experiences in the revelation of the unique environment of a place that appears to them to be sacred. Some of my friends in Bhutan imbue localities with an almost tangible 'spirit of the place' and until a few generations ago, so did many people in this country – some still do. The difference is in the perceptual landscape, the selective acknowledgment of individual aspects of the place that resonate differentially for each person.

The most pervasive myth of all, however, is also the most debilitating. The most profound misunderstanding about land is the myth that 'it doesn't matter who owns the land, it's what they do with it that counts'. A moment of genuine reflection would dismiss that argument completely, for patently the hegemony of landed power has repercussions that have impacted way beyond whether a farmer plants oats or potatoes, or uses the land for sheep, deer, or grouse management. After a conference that I attended in London, the main speakers and the organisers were mingling informally over drinks and nibbles, and I ended up next to a gentleman who identified my Scottish accent and, in a bid to establish some connection, volunteered that he occasionally went shooting on an estate in the Highlands. In the spirit of bridge-building I admitted that I was the owner of an estate in the Highlands and Islands. Oh, (a flicker of interest) how big was my estate? 56,000 acres, I said. Oh, I *say*, that *is* big, Suddenly I was worth conversing with. I neglected to mention that I share my 'ownership' with another 900 residents along the north-western seaboard of the Isle of Lewis in the vigorous and innovative community-owned estate of Urras Oighreachd Ghabhsainn (Galson Estate Trust). In the grand scheme of our lifetime relationship with the land, there is a world of difference between managing the land on the whim of an individual owner and the democratic engagement of a whole community acting for the benefit of that community.

In a similar manner to our lack of knowing about how other people have understood the world about us, that same physical world that we view, we have no way of knowing how the land reacts to us individually, or the ultimate impact that the land and I have upon each other. The question with the currently unknown answer is that if we can forensically detect the chemical signature of the land in the bones of our skeleton thousands of years after we die, (and we can) what impact, if any, does that interaction have upon engendering our affinity to place while we are still alive? Among the many complex, convoluted, and partially-viewed layers of the land, is it more than just a loose metaphor when we occasionally say that someone is 'rooted' in a particular place. To properly understand that, I think, we will need to wait for the progress of science.

# Bibliography

1. ANDERSEN, R., FARRELL, C., GRAF, M., MULLER, F., CALVAR, E., FRANKARD, P., CAPORN, S. and ANDERSON, P. (2017). An overview of the progress and challenges of peatland restoration in Western Europe. *Restoration Ecology* 25 (2) pp 271-282. DOI: https://doi.org/10.1111/rec.12415

2. BEITH, M. (1995). *Healing threads: Traditional medicines of the Highlands and Islands*. Polygon: Edinburgh. ISBN 0-748-66199-9.

3. BELYEA, L.R. and BAIRD, A.J. (2006). Beyond "the limits to peat bog growth": Cross-scale feedback in peatland development. *Ecological Monographs* 76 (3) pp 299-322. https://www.jstor.org/stable/27646045

4. BENNETT, H. (1974-75). A murder victim discovered: clothing and other finds from an early 18th-century grave on Arnish Moor, Lewis. *Proceedings of the Scottish Antiq. Soc.* 106 pp 172-186. http://journals.socantscot.org/index.php/psas/article/download/8918/8886/

5. BENNETT, K.D., BUNTING, M.J. and FOSSITT, J.A. (1997). Long-term vegetation change in the Western and Northern Isles, Scotland. *Botanical J. of Scotland*, 49 (2) pp 127-140. DOI: https://doi.org/10.1080/037466097086848

6. BERRY, W., (1994). *What are people for?* North Point Press: New York. ISBN 0-865-47437-0.

7. BONN, A., REED, M.S., EVANS, C.D., JOOSTEN, H., BAIN, C., FARMER, J., EMMER, I., COUWENBERG, J., MOXEY, A., ARTZ, R., TANNEBERGER, F., VON UNGER, M., SMITH, M-A. and BIRNIE, D. (2014). Investing in nature: Developing ecosystem service markets for peatland restoration. *Ecosystem Services* 9 pp 54-65.

8. BRODY, H. (2002). *Maps and Dreams*. Faber and Faber: London. ISBN 0-571-20967-X.

9. BRODY, H. (1989). *Maps and Journeys*; chapter (pp 133-136 in MacLeod, F. (Ed.) (1989). *Togail Tir: Marking Time: The map of the Western Isles*. Acair and An Lanntair: Stornoway. ISBN 0-86152-842-5.

10. BRONOWSKI, J. (1976). *The Ascent Of Man*. Book Club Associates : London.

11. BROOKE, K. AND WILLIAMS, A. (2021). Iceland as a therapeutic landscape: white wilderness spaces for well-being. *GeoJournal* 86 pp 1275-1285. DOI" https://doi.org/10.1007/s10708-019-10128-9

12. BRUCE, G. and RENNIE, F. (Eds.) (1991). *The Land out there: A Scottish Land Anthology*. Aberdeen University Press: Aberdeen. 342pp. ISBN 0-08-040907-5.

13. BRUCE, G. and SCOTT, P.H. (Ed's.) (2002). *A Scottish post bag: eight centuries of Scottish letters*. The Saltire Society: Edinburgh. ISBN 0-85411-078-X.

14. CALLICOTT, J.B. and NELSON, M.P. (Eds.) (1998). *The great new wilderness debate*. University of Georgia Press: London. ISBN 0-8203-1984-8.

15. CAMPBELL, A. (2013). *Rathad an isean: The bird's road: A Lewis moorland glossary*. ISBN 978-0-9571530-1-1.

16. CHAPMAN, H. (2015). The Landscape Archaeology of bog bodies. *Journal of Wetland Archaeology* 15 (1) pp 109-121. DOI: https://doi.org/10.1080/14732971.2015.1112592

17. CHAPMAN, S., BUTTLER, A., FRANCEZ, A-J., LAGGOUN-DÉFARGE, F., VASANDER, H., SCHLOTER, M., COMBE, J., GROSVERNIER, P., HARMS, H., EPRON, D., GILBERT, D. and MITCHELL, E. (2003). Exploitation of northern peatlands and biodiversity maintenance: a conflict between economy and ecology. *Frontiers in Ecology and the Environment* 1 (10) pp 525-532. DOI: https://doi.org/10.2307/3868163

18. COMUNN EACHDRAIDH NIS (1980). *Leabhar nan comharraidhean*. Comunn Eachdraidh Nis.

19. COMUNN GAIDHEALACH LEODHAIS (1982). *Eilean Fraoich: Lewis Gaelic songs and melodies*. Acair: Stornoway. ISBN 0-86152-052-1.

20. COWIE, T., PICKIN, J. and WALLACE, C. (2011). Bog bodies from Scotland: old finds, new records. *Journal of Wetland Archaeology* 10 (1) pp 1-45. DOI: https://doi.org/10.1179/jwa.2011.10.1.1

21. CRAWFORD, R.M.M. (2001). Plant community responses to Scotland's changing environment. *Botanical J. of Scotland* 53 (2) pp 77-105. DOI: https://doi.org/10.1080/03746600108685016

22. CURRIE, A. (1979). The vegetation of the Outer Hebrides. *Proc. Royal Soc. Edinburgh* 77B, pp 219-265.

23. DARLING, F.F. (Ed.) (1955). *West Highland Survey: An essay in Human Ecology*. Oxford University Press: London.

24. DARLING, F.F. (1970). *Wilderness and Plenty: The Reith Lectures 1969*. Ballantine Books: London. ISBN 345-02159-2.

25. DAVIES, J. (2005a). Uncle Joe knew where you lived. Soviet mapping of Britain (part 1). *Sheetlines* 72 (April) pp 26-38. https://s3.eu-west-2.amazonaws.com/sheetlines-articles/Issue72page26.pdf

26. DAVIES, J. (2005b). Uncle Joe knew where you lived. Soviet mapping of Britain (part 2). Sheetlines 73 (August) pp 6-20. http://www.charlesclosesociety.org/files/Issue73page6.pdf

27. DENVIR, B. (Ed.) (1987). *The Impressionists at first hand*. Thames and Hudson: London. ISBN 0-500-20209-5.

28. DILLARD, A. (1976). *Pilgrim at Tinker Creek*. Pan: London. ISBN 0-330-24715-8.

29. DOUGHTY, K. (2020). Therapeutic landscapes. Chapter 27, pp 341-353 in HOWARD, P., THOMPSON, I., WATERTON, E. and ATHA, M. (Eds.) (2020). *The Routledge Companion to Landscape Studies*. (2nd Edition). Routledge: London. ISBN 978-0-367-73375-9.

30. DUNN, C. and FREEMAN, C. (2011). Peatlands: our greatest source of carbon credits? *Carbon Management* 2 (3) pp 289-301. DOI: https://doi.org/10.4155/cmt.11.23

31. DWELLY, E. (1973). *The illustrated Gaelic to English dictionary*. 8th Edition. Gairm: Glasgow.

32. ERRINGTON, L. (1989). *William McTaggart 1835-1910*. National Gallery of Scotland: Edinburgh. ISBN 0-903148-91-9.

33. FINLAY, J.M. (2018). 'Walk like a penguin': Older Minnesotans' experiences of (non) therapeutic white space. *Social Science and Medicine* 198 pp 77-84. DOI: https://doi.org/10.1016/j.socscimed.2017.12.024

34. FLEET, C., WILKES, M. and WITHERS, W. J. (2012). *Scotland: Mapping the Nation*. Birlinn: Edinburgh. ISBN 978-1-78027-091-3.

35. FLEET, C., WILKES, M. and WITHERS, W. J. (2016). *Scotland: Mapping the Islands*. Birlinn: Edinburgh. ISBN 978-1-78027-351-8.

36. FRIEL, B. (1981). *Translations*. Faber and Faber: London.

37. FRIEL, B. (1989). *From 'Translations'*. In: MacLEOD, F. (Ed.) (1989). *Togail Tir: Marking Time. The map of the Western Isles*, pp 105-111. Acair and An Lanntair: Stornoway. ISBN 0-86152-842-5.

38. GAUDIG, G., FENGLER, F., KREBS, M., PRAGER, A., SCHULZ, J., WICHMANN, S. and JOOSTEN, H. (2014). Sphagnum farming in Germany – a review of progress. *Mires and Peat* 13 Article 8, pp 1-11. https://www.researchgate.net/publication/313218265_Sphagnum_farming_in_Germany-a_review_of_progress

39. GLOB, P.V. (1977). *The Bog People: Iron-Age Man Preserved*. Faber and Faber: London. ISBN 0-571-11079-7.

40. GOLEMAN, D. (2010). *Ecological intelligence.* Penguin: London. ISBN 978-0-141-03909-1.

41. GOODE, D.A. and LINDSAY, R.A. (1979). The peatland vegetation of Lewis. *Proc. Royal Soc. Edinburgh* 77B pp 279-293.

42. GRIGOR, I.F. (1979). *Mightier than a lord: The Highland crofters' struggle for the land.* Acair: Stornoway. ISBN 0-86152-030-0.

43. GUNN, N.M. (1942). *Young Art and old Hector.* Faber and Faber: London.

44. GUNN, N.M. (1988). *The other landscape.* Richard Drew Publishing: Glasgow. ISBN 0-86267-227-9.

45. GUNN, N.M. (1993). *The Atom of Delight.* Polygon: Edinburgh. ISBN 0-7486-6155-7.

46. HALE, W.G. (1988). *The Redshank.* Shire Natural History: Aylesbury. ISBN 0-85263-959-7.

47. HARVIE-BROWN, J.A. and BUCKLEY, T.E. (1888). *A vertebrate fauna of the Outer Hebrides.* D. Douglas: Edinburgh.

48. HILL, M.O. (1992). *Sphagnum: a field guide.* UK Joint Nature Conservation Committee: Peterborough. ISBN 1-873701-14-4.

49. HOWARD, P., THOMPSON, I., WATERTON, E. and ATHA, M. (Eds.) (2020). *The Routledge Companion to Landscape Studies.* (2nd Edition). Routledge: London. ISBN 978-0-367-73375-9.

50. HOWIE, S.A. and HEBDA, R.J. (2018). Bog surface oscillation (mire breathing): A useful measure in raised bog restoration. *Hydrological Processes* 32 pp 1518-1530. DOI: http://doi.org/10.1002/hyp.11622

51. LANGDON, P.G. and BARBER, K.E. (2004). Snapshots in time: precise correlations of peat-based proxy climate records in Scotland using mid-Holocene tephras. *The Holocene* 14 (1) pp 21-33. https://doi.org/10.1191/0959683604hl686rp

52. LEAST HEAT-MOON, W. (1991). *PrairyErth (a deep map)*. Haughtiness Mifflin: Boston. ISBN 0-395-48602-5.

53. LENGEN, C. (2015). The effects of colours, shapes, and boundaries of landscapes on perception, emotion and mentalising processes promoting health and well-being. *Health and Place* 35 pp 166-177. DOI: http://dx.doi.org/10.1016/j.healthplace.2015.05.016

54. LEOPOLD, A. (1949). *A Sand County Almanac and sketches here and there*. Oxford University Press: London. ISBN 978-0-19-500777-0.

55. LOPEZ, B. (1987). *Arctic Dreams*. Pan (Picador): London. ISBN 0-330-29538-1.

56. LOPEZ, B. (2019). *Horizon*. Bodley Head: London. ISBN 978-1-847-92577-0.

57. MacDONALD, M. (2006). Art, Maps and Books: Visualising and Re-visualising the Highlands. https://murdomacdonald.wordpress.com/art-maps-and-books-visualising-and-re-visualising-the-highlands/

58. MacDONALD, M. (2010). Seeing colour in the Gàidhealtachd: An ecology of mind? *Scottish Affairs* 73 pp 1-10.

59. MacDONALD, M. (2013). *Alphabet/Colour/Gaidhealtachd: am ecology of mind*. URL: https://murdomacdonald.wordpress.com/alphabet-colour-gaidhealtachd-an-ecology-of-mind https://murdomacdonald.wordpress.com/alphabet-colour-gaidhealtachd-an-ecology-of-mind/

60. MacDONALD, M. (Ed.) (2019). *Donald Smith: The Paintings of an Islander: Dealbhan le Eileanach*. Acair: Stornoway. ISBN 978-1-78907-043-9.

61. MacDONALD, M. (2020). *Patrick Geddes's Intellectual Origins*. Edinburgh University Press: Edinburgh. ISBN 978-1-4744-5408-7.

62. MacDONALD, M. (2021). *Scottish Art*. Thames and Hudson: London. ISBN 978-0-500-20452-8.

63. MacGREGOR, N. (2010). *A history of the world in 100 objects*. Allen Lane: London. ISBN 978-1-846-14413-4.

64. MacKAY, J.W. (1995). People, perceptions and moorland. Chapter 9 (pp 102-111) in Thompson, D.B.A., Hester, A.J. and Usher, M.B. (Eds.) (1995). *Heaths and Moorland: Cultural Landscapes*. HMSO: Edinburgh. ISBN 0-11-495180-2.

65. MacKAY BROWN, G. (1974). *The two fiddlers*. Chatto and Windus: London. ISBN 0-7011-5041-6.

66. MacLEAN, M. (2021). Living Language Land. https://living-language-land.org/words/aibidil/

67. MacLEAN, R. (MacIlleathain, Ruairidh) (2021). *Ecosystem Services and Gaelic: a scoping exercise.* NatureScot Research Report No. 1230 83pp. https://www.nature.scot/sites/default/files/2021-03/Publication%202021%20-%20NatureScot%20Research%20Report%201230%20-%20Ecosystem%20Services%20and%20Gaelic.pdf

68. MacLEOD, F. (Ed.) (1989). *Togail Tir: Marking Time. The map of the Western Isles.* Acair and An Lanntair: Stornoway. ISBN 0-86152-842-5.

69. MANSFIELD, D.F. (2021). Plimpton 322: A study of Rectangles. *Foundations of Science.* DOI: https://doi.org/10.1007/s10699-021-09806-0

70. MARSHALL, C., BRADLEY, A.V., ANDERSEN, R. and LARGE, D.J. (2021). *Using peatland surface motion (bog breathing) to monitor Peatland Action sites.* NatureScot Research Report 1269. NatureScot: Inverness. https://www.nature.scot/doc/naturescot-research-report-1269-using-peatland-surface-motion-bog-breathing-monitor-peatland-action

71. MARTEN, G.G. (2001). *Human Ecology: basic concepts for sustainable development.* Earthscan Publications: London. ISBN 1-85383-714-8.

72. MATHESON, W. (1964). Murder tradition may explain find. *Stornoway Gazette* Week ending 4 July 1964, p 7.

73. McCLEERY, A. (Ed.) (1987). *Landscape and Light: Essays by Neil M. Gunn.* Aberdeen University Press: Aberdeen. ISBN 0-08-035060-7.

74. McINTOSH, A. (2004). *Soil and Soul: people versus corporate power*. Arum Press: London. ISBN 978-1-85410-942-2.

75. MCINTOSH, A. (2020). *Riders on the storm: The climate crisis and the survival of being*. Birlinn: Edinburgh. ISBN 978-1-78027-639-7.

76. McKIRDY, A. (2018). *The Outer Hebrides: Landscapes in stone*. Birlinn: Edinburgh. ISBN 978-1-78027-509-3.

77. McPHEE, J. (2000). *Annals of the former world*. Farrar, Straus, and Giroux: New York. ISBN 978-0-374-51873-8.

78. McVEAN, D.N. AND RATCLIFFE, D.A. (1962). *Plant communities of the Scottish Highlands: A study of Scottish mountain, moorland and forest vegetation*. Monograph of the Nature Conservancy No. 1. HMSO: London.

79. MELZIG, M. F. and BÖTTGER, S. (2020). Tormentillae rhizoma – Review for an Underestimated European Herbal Drug. *Planta Medica* 86 pp 1050-1057. DOI: https://doi.org/10.1055/a-1129-7214

80. MILLIKEN, W. and BRIDGEWATER, S. (2013). *Flora Celtica: Plants and People in Scotland*. Birlinn and the Royal Botanic Garden Edinburgh: Edinburgh. ISBN 978-1-78027-169-9.

81. MURRAY, J. (1993). *The best of the Group of Seven*. McClelland and Stewart: Toronto. ISBN 0-7710-6674-0.

82. PANKHURST, R. J. and MULLIN, J. M. (1991). *The flora of the Outer Hebrides*.: HMSO: London. ISBN 0-11-310047-7.

83. PARKER PEARSON, M., CHAMBERLAIN, A.T., COLLINS, M.J., CRAIG, O.E., MARSHALL, P., MULVILLE, J., SMITH, H., CHENERY, C., COOK, G., CRAIG, G., EVANS, J., HILLER, J., MONTGOMERY, J., SCHWENNINGER, J-L., TYLOR, G. and WESS, T. (2005). Evidence for mummification in Bronze Age Britain. *Antiquity* 79 (Issue 305) pp 529-546.

84. PEARSALL, W.H. (1989). *Mountains and Moorlands.* (Collins New Naturalist Series). Bloomsbury: London. ISBN 1-870630-53-X.

85. PURSER, J. (2014). The significance of music in the Gàidhealtachd in the Pre- and Early-Historic Period. *Scottish Affairs* 37 pp 207-221. DOI: http://dx.doi.org/10.2218/ss.v37i0.1809

86. RANDALL, J. (2017). *The Historic Shielings of Pàirc.* Islands Book Trust: Laxay, Isle of Lewis. ISBN 978-1-907443-75-6.

87. RENNIE, F. (1998). *Land, culture, and the future of rural communities.* The Lews Castle College Rural Lecture 1998. Stornoway: Lews Castle College ISBN 0-9533808-0-7. Available at: https://www.lews.uhi.ac.uk/t4-media/one-web/lews/research/contact/prof-frank-rennie/prof-frank-rennie-publications/LandCultureandtheFutureofRuralCommunities.pdf

88. RENNIE, F. (2020a). *The changing Outer Hebrides: Galson and the meaning of Place.* Acair: Stornoway. ISBN 978-1-78907-083-5.

89. RENNIE, F. (2020b). Space, Place, and Grace: perceptions of a nisomaniac. Chapter in *Between Islands* pp 33-45. Stornoway: Published by Acair for An Lanntair. ISBN 978-1-78907-084-2.

90. RENNIE, F. (2021). The Corncrake: the ecology of an enigma. Whittles: Dunbeath.

91. RITCHIE, E. (2016). Wild land: alternative insights into Scotland's unpeopled places. https://www.communitylandscotland.org.uk/wp-content/uploads/2017/06/Wild-Land-alternative-insights-into-Scotlands-unpeopled-places-final.pdf

92. ROBERTSON, I. and RICHARDS, P. (Eds.) (2003). *Studying Cultural Landscapes*. Hodder Arnold: London. ISBN 0-340-76268-3.

93. ROTHERHAM, I.D. (2020). *Peatlands: Ecology, Conservation, and Heritage*. Routledge: London. ISBN 978-1-138-34321-4.

94. SANDERSON, J. and HARRIS, L.D. (Eds.) (2020). *Landscape Ecology: A top-down approach*. CRC Press: London. ISBN 978-0-367-57906-7.

95. SHEPHERD, N. (1984) (1977). *The living mountain.* Aberdeen University Press: Aberdeen. ISBN 0-900015-40-3.

96. SMOUT, T.C. (Ed.) (1993). *Scotland since prehistory.* Scottish Cultural Press: Aberdeen. ISBN 1-898218-03-X.

97. SMOUT, T.C. (Ed.) (2001). *Nature, landscape and people since the Second World War.* Tuckwell Press: East Lothian. ISBN 1-86232-147-7.

98. SMOUT, T. C. (2011). *The Highlands and the Roots of Green Consciousness, 1750-1990*. Chapter 2 in *Exploring Environmental History: Selected Essays*. Edinburgh: Edinburgh University Press. ISBN 978-0-7486-4561-9.

99. STEGNER, W. (1993). *Where the Bluebird sings to the lemonade springs: Living and writing in the west.* Penguin Books: London. ISBN 0-14-017402-8.

100. STORNOWAY GAZETTE (1964). *Body found in peat bank.* Week ending 6 June 1964, p1.

101. STORNOWAY GAZETTE (1965). *Peat bank body a victim of murder.* Week ending 23 January 1965, p 1.

102. THOMPSON, D.B.A., HESTER, A.J. and USHER, M.B. (Eds.) (1995). *Heaths and Moorland: Cultural Landscapes.* HMSO: Edinburgh. ISBN 0-11-495180-2.

103. TILLEY, C. (1994). *A phenomenology of landscape: Places, Paths and Monuments.* Berg Publishers: Oxford. ISBN 1-85973-076-0.

104. VITEK, W. and JACKSON, W. (Eds.) (1996). *Rooted in the Land.* Yale University Press: New Haven, USA. ISBN 0-300-06961-8.

105. WALL KIMMERER, R. (2020). *Braiding Sweetgrass.* Penguin: London. ISBN 978-0-141-99195-5.

106. WALL KIMMERER, R. (2021). *Gathering moss: A natural and cultural history of mosses.* Penguin: London. ISBN 978-0-141-99762-9.

107. WHITEFORD, A. (2017). *An enormous reckless blunder: The story of the Lewis Chemical Works.* Islands Book Trust: Laxay, Scotland. ISBN 978-1-907443-74-9.

108. WILKIE, J. (1987). *Metagama: A journey from Lewis to the New World.* Mainstream: Edinburgh. ISBN 1-85158-080-8.